EC. 1985

1987

1 2

3

4

The street in Perugia, **1**, and the square in Nancy, **2**, express not only their geographical differences but also those of their periods in history: **1** is medieval, **2** is Rococo. The differences of towns built at different times are not accidental but the result of deep-seated and deeply felt modes of thought and feeling. They are expressed by the way in which artists see their towns. Their visions sum up the attitudes of their contemporaries and often anticipate and kindle those of the future. Ambrogio Lorenzetti's painting, **3**, dates from about 1340. The town and the countryside around it did not really look like this, both were treated symbolically by the artist, but the intention is unmistakable. The town is seen as a closed system, life goes on only behind the protective wall; beyond it is a near-desert. Because the picture represents the idea of a town, rather than a real town, the artist was able to reduce the number of houses, but in spite of that he has shown us the essential characteristics of the medieval town as he knew it. Note the castle with its separate wall and the typical irregular street pattern of the town. Once again the idea of a natural organism suggests itself, a core of human warmth surrounded by hostile nothingness.

The painting of about 1400 showing Marco Polo's departure from Venice (next page) is also in essence medieval. We can recognise certain features of Venice, for instance St Mark's and its bronze horses on the left, and the two free-standing columns at the end of the Piazzetta, but these, as well as the houses and even the butcher's shop in front of St Mark's, are symbolic, not real. There is no strong sense of place or of space, so that the people (tradesmen, shoppers, city elders, etc.) move uneasily within it. Since the space of the picture is not real it can also take in future events (Marco Polo's journey) and distant lands inhabited by lions, leopards and other strange animals.

Carpaccio, (1455-1526) a Renaissance painter, had quite different ideas about the town. In this miraculous composition, **4**, showing English ambassadors being received by the king, all the essential ingredients of the town, as understood at the time, are shown. There is, on the right, the basic cell of which the town is built: the human habitation within which the more intimate parts of life take place. This is an interior space and the sense of enclosure is tightest in this corner of the picture. In the room next to it, partly enclosed, partly open, proceedings of the highest importance are being enacted. In the colonnade on the extreme left groups of elegant, urbane men are standing about; smaller groups as well as individuals and even animals people the space beyond. Impressive buildings are framed by the state room; other parts of the town can be seen through the gaps in the architecture. Many different moods and conditions of man are depicted here and these are accompanied at each stage by modulations of space ranging from enclosure to open space with suggestions of the outside world. How totally opposed this vision is to the inward-looking medieval one. Here people are moving about in a relationship spatially harmonious to their environment. This picture is a description of the town as a container of all the varied and subtle facets of human life, seen through Renaissance eyes.

mence li liures du grant CHAM qui parole de la grant ermenie de perse
artais et dynde. Et des grauz merueille qui p̃ le mõde sont
Qui sauoir la pure verite des bles cauz nule mensonge. Et chascun qui

Looking and Seeing 4

THE
SHAPE OF
TOWNS

by Kurt Rowland MSIA

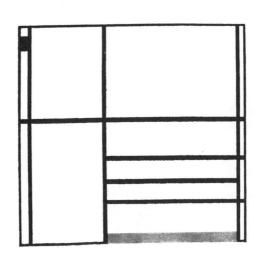

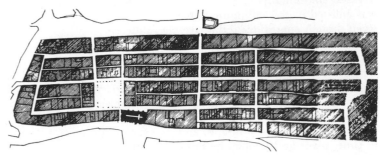

Ginn and Company Ltd

About this book

In the first three parts of *Looking and Seeing* we have examined man-made objects and the many forces and currents which guide their creation. These objects, while they are the outcome of man's reaction to his environment, themselves exert a subtle influence on that environment, on the way we order our lives, on the way we think and feel. The objects do not normally function independently or in isolation; usually they influence each other during the process of creation, even during the process of gestation in their creators' minds. Each one contributes to the total effect of the man-made world on the pattern of our lives.

The face of the town, the townscape, is the most powerful expression of this total effect. As a Greek chorus comments on the action of the play, so this chorus of individually designed objects provides a commentary on the quality of our own lives. In so doing it creates the very conditions in which action may take place and in which human senses may flourish and develop.

At the present time the idea of town planning is in most people's minds. We all know that conditions in towns have reached an impasse, that something drastic will have to be done about urban living: new methods devised, new solutions found, new forms invented. Although there seems to be little unanimity, or even broad agreement, about the nature of these new forms, we all sense that it is more than a matter of making the best use of technological advances, of rationalising building techniques, of smoothing out the flow of traffic. But what more?

If we look at the towns of the past we cannot fail to notice that the change from period to period, from century to century, was far from arbitrary. It was always the crystallisation of what people thought and felt at the time. Every generation built its towns—or made addition to those it had inherited—in its own image. Like other works of art, these towns were efficient not only mechanically but also emotionally. The artist's ordering genius was enlisted in this communal creation.

Even though conditions today are very different, we must still recognise the obvious fact that town design is more than a matter of finding solutions to a number of organisational problems and that it requires above all an artistic solution. The modern designer uses the results of many different kinds of research to solve diverse problems. Through his understanding of the problem, and his sensitivity to time, place and people, he fuses these different elements into one comprehensive design. Mass production has made the design of man-made things more crucial than ever before. Today countless people may be affected adversely by a single designer's miscalculation or insensitivity. In the design of towns this effect is magnified. Industrially produced objects have a limited life and are eventually superseded by new, more efficient objects, but the townscape by its very nature is slow to change. Any mistakes in its design are difficult to eradicate and may spell misery for a generation or more. What is worse they may through their damaging effect on the human organism so stifle or permanently distort the normal exercise of the senses that improvements are neither demanded nor initiated.

That is why the study of town design is important to us all.

© K. F. Rowland 1966
Ninth impression 1981   018109
ISBN 0 602 20612 X

Published by Ginn and Company Ltd
Elsinore House, Buckingham Street, Aylesbury, Bucks HP20 2NQ, U.K.

Printed in Hong Kong by Bookbuilders Ltd

MALINES.

MECHELEN

Contents

Introduction

How do you feel when you wake up in the morning? Do you try to go to sleep again, to withdraw once more into the cosy world from which you are just emerging? But soon you become fully conscious. The outside world is there waiting for you. And somehow, in spite of the comfort of your bed, you want to go out into the world. So you open your eyes again, you sit up, yawn, stretch, perch on the edge of the bed, wash, dress, eat your breakfast, walk to the bus stop, perhaps queue, and finally get on the bus. You are on your way. Life has absorbed you once more.

how many of them you can experience directly. Your breakfast, the view through your window, the streets and houses on your walk to the bus stop, the bus itself, and the all too familiar sight of traffic and the busy town centre, all these you know and they mean something to you. You can touch them, often even smell them. If someone mentions any of these, an image comes into your mind, you remember them as part of your experience. They are in fact your *environment* and the people who fill it are your *community*. In the last picture you can see how one's environment and community may

Waking up is rather like being born. Out of your own private little world of peace and repose, away from the demands and stresses of everyday life, you are projected into reality, and it is sometimes unpleasant. But gradually you find your way back into your familiar environment. If you look at the pictures on this page, you will see that at each successive stage you have taken another step into everyday life, there are gradually more things and more people around you. It is as though ever-increasing circles were being drawn round you, as you experience more and more of your environment.

But when is the limit reached? When does the circle become so large that you can no longer experience everything within it?

Well, look at the pictures again, and decide how many of the objects really mean anything to you,

be experienced on a large scale. You are surrounded by people—outside there are more people, traffic, buildings, life and bustle.

As you open your newspaper and read today's most important headlines, how do they strike you? They probably deal mostly with national issues, perhaps even international ones; there may be news of a government reshuffle, or of the visit of a foreign statesman, but these events will be farther removed from your everyday experience than all the things going on around you. You may understand the things and ideas you read about in the newspaper, but you probably don't experience them as strongly as the things in your immediate environment. The increasing circles of your

travel each morning to get to their fields. Nor could towns exist until farmers were able to produce a surplus, that is to say, more than they and their families required. This surplus could feed a number of people who did not till the soil: specialists of various kinds, such as toolmakers, builders, weavers, potters, scholars. These townspeople were normally dependent on each other's skills; the carpenter, for instance, required tools which only a toolmaker could manufacture, and the builder in his turn required the carpenter's highly skilled work. In this way, as time went by, the town grew into a most complex organism, in which each member depended on one or more of the others, and the town could exist

environment: bed, room, house, street, town—these are part of your immediate experience. Beyond that—England, Europe, the world—you have to make a mental effort to understand. The town then is the largest environment which comes within your experience. It is the largest community which can involve each member in a *direct* way. That is why the town has always played a most important part in history.

There was a time when people were much more evenly spread over the face of the earth than they are now. People settled where the soil was fertile, but they could not live too closely together because each family had to have a certain area of land to support it. The size of villages was kept down by the fact that the surrounding land would feed only so many mouths, and the more people lived together in one place the farther they had to

only by maintaining this finely balanced state. A town can be compared to a natural organism, such as a plant, in which many different things are going on at the same time, and in which each part is dependent on the others. And, like a natural organism, the town took in a number of materials, raw materials and ideas, and in the process of living converted them into a different set of materials. The town became the most impressive large-scale organism in existence. In it a man could feel and express himself as an individual yet, from time to time, become part of something larger, pursuing activities, and savouring qualities of life, which in his purely individual state, in isolation, would be denied him. The town therefore expresses man's dual role. It is in fact the largest visual manifestation of man as an individual and as a communal being.

But these abstract thoughts about the town do not
seem to tally with what you actually see going on
around you. Things somehow do not seem to be
working with the smoothness one associates with
the functioning of an organism. As the bus stops
the people getting off clash with those trying to
get on. As you cross the road you have to take very
great care not to be knocked down by passing
vehicles. Cars, lorries, vans, buses, motor cyclists
going in different directions have effectively blocked
each other's paths, and farther down the road the
traffic has in fact come to a standstill. You get a
momentary feeling that people are against each
other and not, as in your ideal town, supporting
each other. This is further confirmed as you walk
from the bus stop to your destination. There are
lorries trying to park in impossibly small spaces
in order to unload their wares. The workshops for
which some of the loads are intended are located
round a small courtyard. People living in the
surrounding buildings have to endure the noise of
the machines as well as of the lorries and the smells
which result from the presence of a factory.
Telephone and electrical wires of all kinds, lamps,
road-signs, hoardings all add an element of confusion
which would be all the more disturbing if we were
not used to this kind of neighbourhood. In such
environments the individual person can hardly
be said to live the ideal life in which he can express
himself fully, nor does present-day town life
encourage close communities in which the individual
can find his place. The modern town works largely
against the individual and the community—or at
any rate it provides less than ideal conditions for
either. And yet the idea of an ideal town seems so
perfectly reasonable that one cannot understand
why it should not exist. Can it be that in the modern
world the town as it existed in history is becoming
not only impossible but even unnecessary?
There are many reasons why towns have changed
their character. For example, people move about
from place to place much more than they used to
and they may have lost some of their local pride.
Television and private transport have isolated each
individual from his neighbours so that communal
facilities are not nearly as important as they used
to be. But before we abandon the idea of the
town altogether, or decide to reconstitute it, we
must enquire into the real character of the town in
history, into its purpose and the human needs it
served. We must also try to find out why towns
ever grew up at all and what determined their
appearance.

1 The medieval town

During the Dark Ages and the unsettled times which followed it was natural that the weak should seek the protection of the strong and that the strong should then become the rulers. Often these rulers took over from the Roman administrators who had governed the district before. Sometimes kingdoms became too large for a king to govern effectively, and then local lords set themselves up under the king. Everywhere knights' castles rose, **1**, as visible signs of the new order, *feudalism*. The knight's armed retainers gave protection to the people of the surrounding district and in return for this protection the land and everything on it belonged to the knight. But there was also another power in existence: the Church, chiefly represented by the monasteries. Often built on mountain tops or other inaccessible places, away from the usual routes of invading tribes, **2**, monasteries were inhabited by monks who led a life which was self-sufficient and strikingly dissimilar from that of the people around them. At a time when peasants knew only how to provide themselves with sufficient food for their own meagre needs and for the payments of taxes to the lord, there were people living in monasteries who could write and illuminate holy books, write poetry and compose music, carve in stone and metal. The monasteries too owned some of the land.

2 *Mont St. Michel, France and the walled town which grew around it*

Dominated by one of these two powers, feudalism and the Church, the peasant had a tough time. He was a serf, tied to land which he was not allowed to leave. If the land passed from one lord to another—as part of a business transaction or through violence—the serf was considered part and parcel of the land. He worked for his lord in exchange for a strip of land. He paid taxes in any form which his lord commanded. If he ran away, his lord was allowed to pursue him for four days and bring him back in chains, and punish him by beating and whipping, although more severe penalties were often inflicted. He was not allowed to marry without the lord's consent, for which he had to pay a fee. In the event of the serf's death the lord was entitled to take his best possession, perhaps a cow or a pig; the church took the second best. The serf's superiors had a low opinion of him, expressed in such a statement as: 'The peasant deserves to be fed on straw, thistles and thorns, beechmast and acorns, like the swine that he is.' Life was deemed unchangeable, social betterment not desirable. Knights sometimes complained about 'those who will not stay in that state of life to which they were born', and even the Church held that 'Christ came to change men's hearts, not their conditions of life'.

Round about the ninth century signs of change began to appear, a change which, however, did not become general for about two hundred years. It may be that with the passing of the year 1000, which had long been thought to mark the end of the world, people heaved a sigh of relief and began to see life in a new way. It may be that the armed retainers of the local lord were not always wholly successful in defending and protecting the district under his rule. Perhaps people found that even a simple stockade gave them a fair measure of protection from marauders, since powerful machines of war were not commonly in use. A wall was even safer. So instead of relying on the walls of the lord's castle for protection in time of danger, they began to fortify their villages. This they soon found to be far more effective than their lord's protection; it also gave them a little independence. The people began to realise that by banding together and taking their destinies into their own hands they could defend themselves not only against an attacker from without, but sometimes even against the lord himself. Because life inside a fortified place was more orderly and secure, craftsmen and merchants gathered within it and the town was born.

Not all towns began in this way. Some, for instance, arose in places where kings fortified certain points of their realms.

The idea of living together behind fortified walls took hold of men's minds and by the eleventh century a town-building movement was beginning. Some lords, more far-seeing than others, supported the new movement, actually helped in the building of new towns and allowed their castles to become part of the fortifications. They had no advanced democratic ideas, but they must have seen that a new way of life was in the making, and that by moving with the current they might derive some benefits from it in the form of increased taxes. Abbots likewise encouraged townships to grow up round their monasteries for the greater glory of Christianity. But many knights and even abbots opposed the growth of towns because they saw in them a threat to their wealth and power. The struggle between the town and the feudal system was often accompanied by violence and bloodshed. In the end the towns won, but on their path to independence every single achievement had to be fought for. Even after a charter was granted to a town and the inhabitants were allowed to hold markets, to issue their own coins and to be tried in their own courts of justice instead of the lord's court, every townsman knew that he could live only as a member of a community. The community had power, the individual was comparatively insignificant. With

1

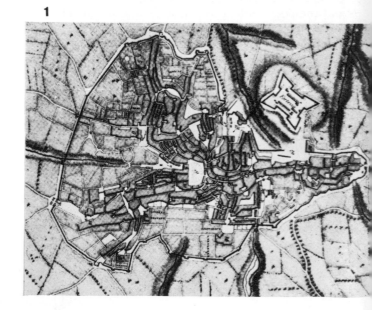

1 *Siena, Italy*
2 *Lucignano, Italy. The contours of the countryside determined the shape of these towns and the pattern of their streets*
3 *Montreal, France. A planned town*

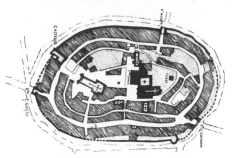

2

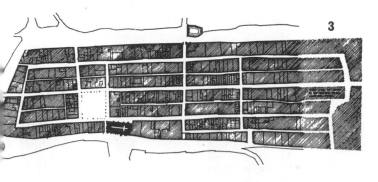

3

the development of the town a new element was added to medieval society, a new class of people: the burghers. They had different values from the landowners and the peasants and also different interests.

From a defensive point of view the site of a town was of the greatest importance. A suitable hilltop, **2**, or the bend of a river, **4**, were considered ideal, but we also find towns which grew round a crossroads, a ford, or a bridge. It was natural that a town should take advantage of every suitable feature in the land on which it was built. Because the town took so much of its character from the nature of the land, it generally fitted into the landscape and became an integral part of it. Streets often followed the contours of the ground on which the town was built or the curvature of the river which enveloped it. The town derived its visual character from the natural feature which gave rise to it—hill, river-bend, ford, bridge, crossroads. Planned towns, **3**, however, were regular in layout.

4

5

6

4 *Shrewsbury, a town making use of contours and river bend*
5 *Ancona, Italy. Street pattern derived from hill and harbour*
6 *Houses and streets are harmoniously related to the ground*

1

2

3

The building materials were those normally found on the spot or nearby. The early town developed a harmonious relationship with its surroundings not only through its overall shape and the layout of its streets but also because the streets and the houses which lined them depended on the natural resources of the region. As only materials found in the immediate neighbourhood of the town could be used, such a town had a harmonious, unified appearance, for all the houses had similar structures, colours and textures. This natural harmony was reinforced by the simple fact that the townspeople could not indulge in any unnatural or artificial methods of building. Often each family would build its own house, helped perhaps by the neighbours, and had to use the most logical methods which combined its needs with the materials available.

Not many examples of those early towns exist today, but we can find odd corners which, although no longer in their original state, still offer examples of the principles of early town building. Many old towns in Italy, such as Gubbio, **1**, Assisi, **2**, and Siena, **3**, were built of stone throughout, but the colour of the stone varies and gives each of these towns its own character, which is directly derived from the nature of the surrounding country. The pictures also show how closely the arrangement of the houses is related to the uneven ground. In parts of Northern Europe, where there was no good building stone but where clay for brickmaking was available, brick houses were built, normally with a timber frame, **4**, **5**. A town set in chalk country would contain mostly flint houses with plaster rendering.

4

5

1

2

3

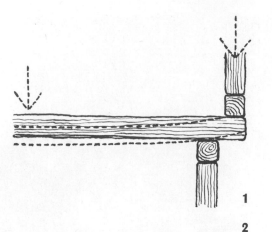

The structure of houses depended on the methods evolved for the different building materials. For instance, in stone districts the arch is much in evidence because this is a most effective way of using stone. Where half-timbered brick buildings were erected a method of allowing the upper storeys to overhang the lower ones was gradually evolved. Such houses look 'quaint' to us today, but we do not always realise that they were built in this form for purely practical purposes. As the diagram, **1**, shows, the jutting out of the beam counteracted the tendency of the beam to sag in the middle. The weight of the outer wall was used to balance the weight of people and furniture inside the house. Like the arcaded walks of stone-built houses, the overhang also served, as glass was both scarce and costly, to protect the lower floor, often an open shop front. Picture **2** shows a medieval shop front, now somewhat restored. The common sense and logic of the structure, with its overhanging upper storey, are evident; it may also have had wooden shutters hinged to the window ledge, which let down to form a counter. Everywhere materials and structures were used in a straightforward and knowledgeable way. Supporting arches not only helped structurally, they also formed visual harmonising links between houses, **3**. Although each item of the medieval townscape was produced individually to suit each individual owner, although houses were often irregularly grouped and did not line up, they were yet held together by all that they had in common, not least by the sense of values which the inhabitants held in common. For, apart from the sheer necessity of building in the most natural and logical way, the inhabitants of early towns were very conscious of belonging to a community, in which each member played a necessary part. A street of medieval houses expresses this awareness. Not only the larger community of the town, but also the smaller and more immediate one of the neighbourhood was expressed visually. Small open spaces and squares, often little more than a broadening of the street, with a central fountain or well, **4**, acted as focal points for small groups of families. The fountain was a necessity, but it also served as a place where people met and chatted. These spaces were linked by short streets which also had a community feeling and so formed a network of small interdependent communities within the larger community of the town, **5**. By and large these interlinked spaces were fairly equal in importance and in status, rather like the cells of a natural organism. This cellular character of the early medieval town was an essential ingredient and persisted for a very long time; it was part of the medieval way of thinking. Houses were similar in character for reasons we have already discussed, and the open spaces which they enclosed likewise fell into a pattern which was repetitive, yet never exactly so. The social pattern of the town, the guilds in which the town's inhabitants were organised, was constructed in a similar way, i.e. in individual parts which were linked up to form a whole. We have discussed patterns of this kind (Part One, Pattern and Shape) and found that they meet a basic human need. From many points of view, the early town provided a harmonious environment for its inhabitants, a harmonious pattern of related houses and interlinked open spaces, applied to the pattern of the country on which it stood and derived from the raw materials it contained. A closer harmony between the man-made and the natural world can hardly be imagined.

If we look at a map of a medieval town, such as Malines (Mechelen) in Belgium, **6**, its true nature becomes obvious. A river runs through it and feeds a whole system of canals, which served as a second means of transport. Streets and canals can be seen to form two intertwined patterns. They are independent of each other but often unite. The curved course of the canals, which was for convenience, as in this form they could be made to serve a larger area, is followed by many streets. The blocks of houses outlined by streets and canals are harmoniously related. There are open spaces which fit into the overall pattern. To compare the overall pattern and structure of a medieval town to that of a natural organism such as **7**, a seed-box, is not at all far fetched, for both are the outcome of a process of natural growth.

4

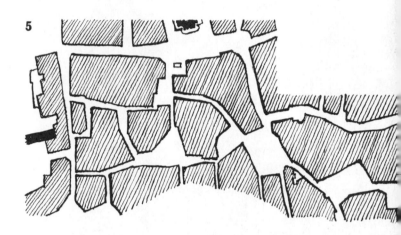

5

6

7

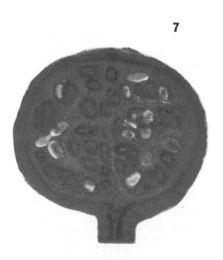

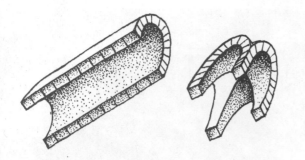

1

2

It was natural in times of great unrest that the church should be the centrepiece of the town, an indication of the position it enjoyed in the life of the townspeople. The buildings and the institutions of the town may have seemed rather new and untried when towns were young, but the Church had been in existence longer than anyone could remember, and could supply answers to many of the questions which ordinary people might ask about life and death. Furthermore, in the initial stages of a town's history at any rate, the only people within the town who could write and keep the town's affairs in order were often the men of the Church.

In the life of the town the Church had many parts to play, apart from the obvious one of providing a place of worship. It certainly also took part in non-religious activities. It was not unusual for deeds of property to be placed in the church building for safe-keeping, or for arms to be stored there. People did not think it unseemly to convert a whole cathedral into a temporary dining hall to feed the crowd at some festivity. There were no theatres but people could watch miracle plays in front of the cathedral doors, usually performed by a cast of both clergy and laymen. As the activities of the Church spread into almost every aspect of town life, the building became a symbol of the town's spirit of independence, and was therefore given pride of place.

Whilst most dwelling houses had to be built from the materials found in the neighbourhood of the town, the church and civic buildings, for which greater resources were available, could make use of stone and other materials brought from afar. The method of building employed was normally that derived from the Romans. There were still many Roman buildings in those parts of Europe which had once been ruled by Rome, some must still have been in use, although no longer for their original purposes, and there were still builders about who understood and practised the Roman building methods. But the Roman barrel vault, as shown in diagram **1**, underwent certain changes. In the structure of the medieval church, **4**, we can see once more the medieval 'cellular' mode of expression. In the same way as house was added to house in the medieval street, street to street and square to square to make a medieval town, and guild to guild to make a town's community, so in building the church vault was added to vault to make a whole, sometimes of enormous dimensions. The heavy walls required to carry the heavy, solid vaults were an appropriate expression of the solid and eternal faith which the church represented, **2, 3**. A large cathedral such as the one at Speyer in Germany is almost overpowering in its simple grandeur, but even such great buildings often had

3

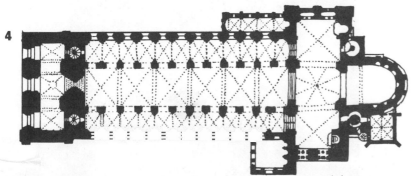

4

2 *Worms cathedral, Germany*
3, 4 *Speyer cathedral, Germany*

1

2

3

touches which made them intimate and human.
Often the capitals of the columns would be
decorated with scenes from the Scriptures, the
history or the life of the town, or the activities of
its inhabitants, **1**. Small parish churches could be
built in the same architectural idiom, a way of
building based on the same values. At Kilpeck
church in Herefordshire, **3**, there are a host of small
sculptures which decorate the structure of the
church, **4**. They are mostly unrealistic and fanciful,
expressing human emotions and the mason's
affection for the materials he uses, qualities which
are seldom found in later sculpture. For instance,
the right-hand corbel in picture **5** expresses love
in a direct human way, a feeling made into stone.
The medieval mason was not particularly concerned
with realism. He was a craftsman, who was vitally
involved with the things he made and who also
wanted to give vent to his fantasies and feelings,
his fears and desires. He therefore expressed those
feelings in a way wholly suited to the materials he
used and to the structure of the church. The
elongated figure, **2**, is another example from
Kilpeck. Like the town itself and the houses of which
it was composed, the medieval church gave an
impression of harmony, humanity, and honesty.

Although materials for civic and religious buildings could be brought from farther afield, there was still a limit to the distance, and churches, even when they were not made of the same materials as the rest of the town, yet reflected the character of the *region* in their materials. In Tuscany, Romanesque churches have a character all their own due to the great mineral wealth of the region. These churches were often decorated in marbles of many colours. The plain of Lombardy, on the other hand, is poor in building stone, and churches in this region were normally built of brick. In the Auvergne, in France, volcanic stone gives the churches their special character. Climatic considerations also play a most decisive part in the appearance of buildings. In southern countries windows are kept small to keep out glare and heat; in the north larger windows are used to admit more light. Roofs in northern countries are more steeply pitched than in the south, to allow snow and rain to drop off. The pictures of Pistoia cathedral in Tuscany, **6**, and Worms cathedral in Germany, page 14, demonstrate these points. In this way not only the town itself, its houses and streets, but also its central and most important building, the church, were in harmony with the surrounding countryside, the materials it produced, and its climate.

As towns grew more prosperous they not only gained in prestige but also became more populous. This map of Bruges, **1**, shows how the town expanded between the eleventh and thirteenth centuries. Many other towns grew at a similar rate. To accommodate the larger congregations, to give their towns a more imposing church or cathedral, and at the same time to save material and labour, the cathedral builders were constantly looking for better and newer methods of construction. The earlier cathedrals were built when craftsmanship was still quite primitive. Masons had neither the skill nor the tools to cut their stones accurately; they were rough-hewn, **2**, and could not be relied upon to grip each other when built into a wall.

But now, in the more settled conditions of town life, masons like other craftsmen could develop their crafts and pass them on to their apprentices to be further developed and perfected. Each mason took a pride in his work. Often he would carve his personal mark on some of the stones which he had shaped, **3**, as a sign of satisfaction with his work. The job of a mason became a highly skilled occupation, and really good master masons were always in demand and travelled far and wide. Because of the great skill which they had acquired, they were able to cut stones more accurately so that the resultant walls were stronger or, alternatively, could be made thinner though just as strong. By adding short cross-walls, called buttresses, which bore most of the weight of the roof, the walls could be made thinner still. But what is more important, their craftsmanship enabled masons to devise new methods of vaulting which were to have far-reaching consequence. Instead of making a vault of heavy masses of stone, as in the earlier, Romanesque churches, they placed finely and accurately chiselled pieces of stone on end to form self-supporting ribs, **4**. The open spaces could then be filled with thin pieces of stone, **5**. Rib-vaulting not only made building itself easier, but saved a great deal of material.

Other difficulties of vaulting still remained and how these were dealt with is described on pages 56-58 of Part 2.

1

The areas shown black are the old castle and the original town. The solid line marks the boundary of the eleventh century town, the dotted line of the twelfth century town.

2

3

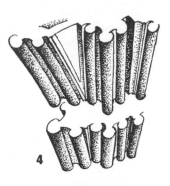

5

6 *Cologne cathedral, Germany*

6

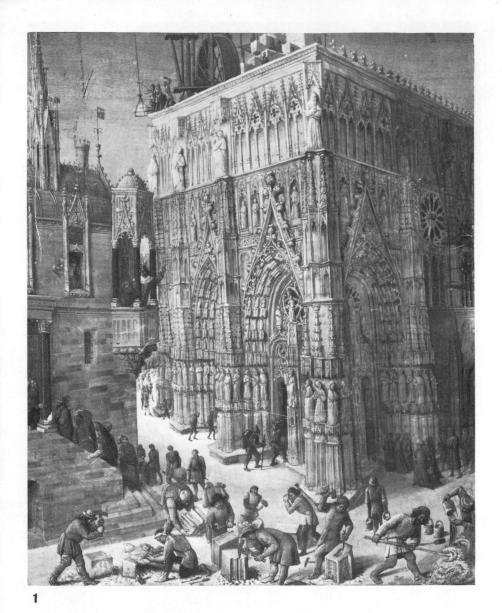

1

4

2

Basically the Gothic building methods were followed over most of Europe, but as always there were local variations. Roofs still remained steeper in the north, windows smaller in the south. In the Northern countries of Europe, the new large windows gave rise to traceried designs of stone to span them and to hold the panels of glass. Now the art of stained glass developed which could decorate the church with stories from the Bible and illuminate it with the mysterious light which is such an essential part of the Gothic cathedral. In southern countries, although Gothic cathedrals were built in great numbers, the spirit of the Gothic was never properly understood. As thick walls with small windows are more effective in keeping out excessive heat, the builders of, for instance, Southern Italy would have seen little point in adopting the northern system which would have given them thin walls with large windows. Traceries and stained glass never became, for this reason, dominant in those parts of Europe. In a northern Gothic cathedral the steep roof was an important element in the design and could be seen from afar. It was a fitting crown to the many verticals, which expressed the devout spirit of the Gothic. But in southern countries the roof was, for climatic reasons, kept flat, and did not play a very prominent part in the design of the church. In the slanting rays of the northern sun vertical features cast the most pronounced shadows, but in the south, due to the more vertical rays of the sun, it is the horizontal features of buildings, such as cornices, which are the most conspicuous. The vertical character of northern Gothic is therefore less important in the south, where it could not look at its best. These reasons ensured a division of the Gothic style into southern and northern. The larger wall spaces of southern churches gave mosaic workers and painters the opportunity to develop their crafts and their vision. The pictures of the cathedrals at Winchester, **5**, and Florence, **3**, **4**, show these points quite clearly. Because municipal buildings closely followed the methods employed in the building of churches, they too show regional differences. The town hall at Volterra, **6**, has small windows with pointed arches, but the cornices give the whole building a horizontal emphasis. The roof cannot be seen. The town hall of Bruges, **7**, has large windows, a strong vertical emphasis and a high roof which forms an essential part of its appearance and character.

5   **6**

7

1

2

3

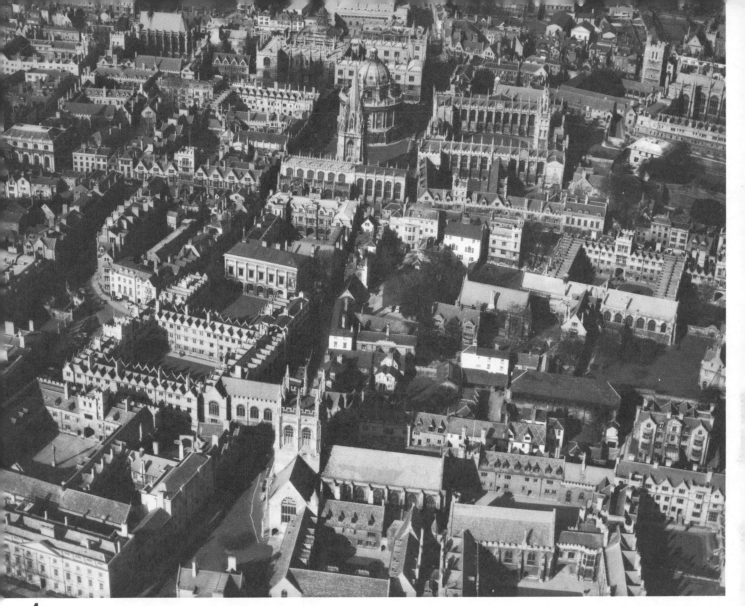

4

But whatever local differences there may have been, the basic medieval manner of thinking and feeling was common throughout Europe. Picture **2** shows a part of a later medieval town, Amsterdam. The merchants' houses are more elaborate than the houses of an earlier medieval town, **1**; they are also larger, for they must incorporate in their design the extensive storehouses of their owners. But they still have a harmonious family resemblance. They are individual units forming a larger unit, an enclosed space. Medieval Oxford is built on the same principle. The modern photograph, **4**, shows that the old layout of streets and enclosures is

1 *Monpazier, France. The varied, interlinked spaces are clearly visible*

3 *The irregular pattern of a medieval town*

still retained, although many buildings have been rebuilt since medieval times. Many of the enclosures are not public spaces, they belong to the various colleges of the university, but they are still expressive of medieval thought and feeling.

In the end the prosperity of the town proved to be the downfall of the medieval way of thinking, feeling and living. This came about as the result of a number of different movements which, as they all converged, brought the medieval period to an end. Many rich families of merchants and bankers had been produced by the prosperity of the late medieval era. The spiritual significance of the Gothic was no longer sufficient for these people, who dealt in material wealth. They loved the good things in life, their houses had become more sumptuous than those of their forebears in the early medieval town, and they required objects with reality of life, which in a town bustling with trade, manufacturing and banking, had assumed an ascendancy over more spiritual and religious ideas. If a rich man donated an altarpiece to his church he would often ask the artist to include his likeness alongside those of the saints and other holy figures in the picture. The donor would insist on a good likeness so that people looking at the picture would be able to recognise him. It was through such needs that ordinary people and artists began to see the world as something real, rather than something imagined, as in earlier times. These changes took place throughout Europe. The statue of Queen Uta in Naumburg Cathedral, **1**, made in the thirteenth century, looks different from the sculpture of a hundred years before in several respects. The figure has detached itself from its architectural setting. It is no longer merely a part of the fabric of the church, but exists in its own right. The artist has observed reality: Uta's pose is typical of a certain type of person, and we would not be hard put to it to identify her with someone we know, so well is her character expressed. People, in short, are now considered in their own right, as individuals.

We have seen that the Gothic cathedral was the outcome, perhaps the flower, of the medieval town, and it was the cathedral which accommodated all the other arts within itself; it was in the cathedral and for the cathedral that all the important artistic experiments, without which there can be no evolution of art, were carried out. But now, at the end of the Middle Ages, the character of the town began to change. Principalities, dukedoms and kingdoms emerged and clipped the independence of the towns, but the towns did not resist as of old because they were no longer such tight communities. New manufacturing processes had made it necessary to move the workshops outside the confines of the town and workers who were not members of the guilds had to be employed. In the meantime the guilds themselves had degenerated. Instead of the old system of apprenticeships which ensured that only the best workers became masters, the son now more usually inherited his father's position, and this meant that inefficient people were sometimes in authority. And as the guilds lost prestige and power, so international business became more important, contributing still more to the eclipse of the town, based as it was on local guilds and not on national or even international connections. The medieval town did not adapt itself to the new social and political conditions in Europe; it was eroded from within and crushed from without. It was natural that its appearance should also change as a result of the new conditions.

1

2 The Renaissance town

The pulpit of Siena cathedral, **1**, is decorated with a number of panels illustrating scenes from the New Testament, dating from 1266-68. The figures are treated with a great deal of realism, they are not mere symbols as was the sculpture of the earlier Middle Ages, but the relationships between them have not been properly understood. In other words the artist has looked at individual figures in real life (and also at Roman sculpture) but he has not yet learned to look at them all together as one comprehensive view: as one group standing in a field or on a hill. They are crowded together in an impossibly small space and seem to be unaware of each other's presence. They are individuals added together, like the houses and so much else in the medieval town. Although they are seen as *real* people, they do not seem to inhabit a *real* world when added together. This total reality was obviously beyond the medieval mind and power of expression, it was outside the medieval visual language.

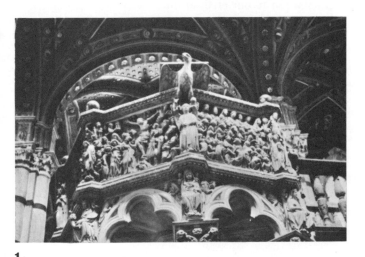

1

If we look at the interior of Siena cathedral, a Gothic building, **2**, we notice a strange use of building materials; marble of different colours has been used to pattern the columns with horizontal bands. Now Gothic, as we have seen, is essentially vertical, pillars, vaults, buttresses, pinnacles, and roofs combining to give it its soaring quality. In the north, where the Gothic spirit was more at home, much was done to stress this quality—columns, for instance, were fluted to create an intense feeling of upward movement. But here the building materials were used to produce a pattern which runs counter to the very nature of the Gothic. Outside we notice similar patterns on the side walls and even on the belltower, **3**. Horizontal cornices run right across the facade, which is crowded with naturalistically carved figures and beasts thrusting forward, away from the face of the church. All these things lead

2

3

away from the Gothic spirit, which was so representative of the medieval world, and point to the fact that new developments are likely to come from this part of Europe. In the north the medieval way of looking at life was still entrenched, but here, in Tuscany, conditions were ripe for the discovery of reality in our sense of the word.

And it was indeed in Tuscany that reality was discovered. Giotto, (1266-1336), one of the greatest artists in the whole history of Western art, took a vital part in this movement and he played his part in such a striking and original way that his contemporary, the poet Petrarch, exclaimed that Giotto could make us believe that things were real when in fact they were only painted. Giotto achieved this unprecedented effect by clarifying the shapes he saw around him. In medieval pictures people and things were flat shapes, ideas of things rather than real things. But Giotto realised that objects appear to us as they do because of the light which catches their surfaces. He therefore explained the things in his pictures in terms of light and shade; this was called *chiaroscuro*. It was the first step towards realism in art. Now it became possible to describe character and emotions in a way which can be recognised as real, **1**.

Equally important in Giotto's work is his realisation of the *relationship* between people and their environment. If you look at a medieval painting or drawing, **2**, you will see at once that the background is of little consequence to the artist— in fact it does not exist. But if you wish to describe the reality of the world, not only people but also the things around them, houses, trees, fields and mountains must be shown. What is more they must be in a natural *relationship* towards each other, they must add up to a whole network of relationships, similar to those we find in the real world, seen as one large unity. Whereas in a medieval painting everything took place in the plane of the picture, now the composition must be three-dimensional in space; some people will be in the foreground, some in the background, and they must be logically linked by the middle distance. In other words it is not enough for a painter to model things in the round, and by means of light and shade, to describe the solid forms. He must also consider the *space* between them; he must see this space also as *form*, but *negative form*, whereas the shapes of real things may be described as *positive form*. We can sense this attempt to see and understand space in Giotto's work, often in the form of architectural structures, which *contain and model* space, so that the people in his pictures can be seen to move in a space which we can understand. This was Giotto's great contribution to our civilisation.

1

Masaccio took this great discovery a stage further. In this picture of the Crucifixion, **3**, painted in 1425, he has devised an architectural setting which has a great feeling of depth and of reality. But he has done more than that. By choosing a low eye level, so that we feel we are looking up at the people

in the picture, he has made sure that we, the onlookers, would place ourselves in a definite spatial relationship to the people in the picture. In other words he has drawn us into the picture so that we can almost imagine that we are taking part in it. We are conscious of the space in which the Crucifixion takes place, and the space between us and the picture. This idea of space as a thing to be reckoned with was the great discovery of the Renaissance. It was sensed by Giotto, taken up and developed by Masaccio and the other great artists of the period following.

The great originality of Masaccio's picture lies in the arrangement of the Roman barrel vault, which draws our eye into the depth of the picture instead of allowing it to roam over the surface, as in a medieval painting. We must remember that Masaccio had never seen such an architectural feature used in this way and for this purpose. Brunelleschi, one of the great Renaissance architects, had already discovered space in his own way, but he was still in some respects Gothic in spirit, just as Giotto was still a Gothic painter. In his church of San Lorenzo in Florence, **4**, there is an awareness of space which we do not normally find in Gothic churches. The flat ceiling and horizontal cornices keep the eye down, instead of taking it upward as in Gothic churches, so that the slender pillars can lead the eye into the distance. At the same time we are aware of the subsidiary spaces of the aisles, which are separated from the nave by nothing more than the rows of slender, graceful columns, which hardly interfere with the *whole* negative form, the whole space enclosed by the church.

4

The difference between San Lorenzo and a northern Gothic church is not superficial, it is fundamental. In a truly medieval church the eye is never allowed to take in the whole of the vista before it. Its attention is constantly attracted by subdivisions of the whole, by details, by the wealth of ornaments, as in a medieval street. The eye is meant to roam from detail to detail, from item to item, but never to conceive the whole in one total vision. But in San Lorenzo we can see all the shapes of which the structure of the church is composed with a clarity which is quite new; we can also understand the structure as one unity. We are made aware not only of the solid shape but also of the negative form which it encloses, the volume of air, space.

In the Pazzi chapel Brunelleschi gave further expression to this new total visual experience. You can see from the photographs, **2, 3**, how carefully the walls, arches, pilasters and other planes have been related to each other and how clear the overall shape is; the best view is obtained from the centre of the building, and this is where the observer is inclined to place himself. The architect, by suggesting a definite point of view for the observer, draws him into a spatial relationship with the chapel. He is made to feel the volume of space within the chapel and through it he becomes involved with the building. Brunelleschi did in architecture something similar to what Masaccio did in painting.

The Pazzi chapel is one of the earliest examples of Renaissance architecture; its importance and influence were very great indeed, but it still betrays medieval modes of thought. The porch of the chapel has a barrel vault, but this is arranged parallel to the front, **5** with a small cupola over the entrance, **4**, and not, as in Masaccio's painting, in our line of sight so as to suggest depth. When Alberti designed the church of St. Andrea in Mantua the façade showed a use of the barrel vault which is rather similar to that in Masaccio's painting. Unlike the one on the front of the Pazzi chapel, it draws the eye into the building. This church was designed in 1472. It is strange to think that architectural features should have been anticipated by a painter by about fifty years.

1

2

1 *Another view of San Lorenzo*
6 *St. Andrea, Mantua, Italy*

3   **4**

5   **6**

1

2

3

The bronze doors of the baptistery of Florence
give us a good insight into the process of the
discovery of the real world. There are three pairs
of doors; all of them bear low relief panels depicting
scenes from the Bible. The first pair was designed by
Andrea Pisano in 1330. The second by Ghiberti
in 1404, completed in 1424, the third, also by
Ghiberti was not completed until 1452. The three
pictures show one panel from each of these doors.
You will see that the figures gradually become more
life-like. Pisano's figures are still fairly stiff.
Ghiberti's of 1404 are considerably more natural,
and in the last pair of doors they burst out of their
frames and invade the decorative border. But not
only do the figures themselves become more real;
perhaps the most important aspect of this progression
is that the relationship between people and
background becomes more realistic. In the first
panel the background is reduced to a mere symbol.
The comparison with the last panel is most striking;
here the people can be seen in a spatial
relationship to the background. Ghiberti's is a
more real world than Pisano's.

The statue of St. George by Donatello, **5**, is in
many ways typical of the fifteenth century. This is
the fearless ideal of Renaissance man, standing on
his own two feet. There is no uncertainty here,
only affirmation. This figure has a solidity and
appearance of physical weight quite unknown
to earlier sculptors. Whilst late Gothic sculptors
sought to portray elegance, Renaissance sculptors
looked for reality, even if it was less pretty.

4

1 *Andrea Pisano*
2 *Ghiberti*
3 *Ghiberti*
4 *Detail from the last pair of doors by Ghiberti*
6 *In this Renaissance drawing, showing an actor on a stage, the buildings are related to each other and to the actor, by means of perspective.*

Drawing the eye into the scene (whether the scene was a picture painted on a wall or on canvas, or a real one in the form of a building) was too important to be left to chance; it had to be worked out as a system, for only then could it be used universally. This new system was called *perspective;* it became an important tool in the hands of the artist and an important element in the visual language of the Renaissance.

To the artist—painter, sculptor, or architect—perspective was of the utmost importance. It gave him a method of exploring spatial relationships with a mathematical precision. It was a tool for investigating the world of reality, which the Renaissance had discovered. To a medieval artist perspective would have been useless; space as such did not mean anything to him; a total vision of reality was outside his imagination. Perspective was invented because it was needed for the first time. It belongs wholly to the mental climate of the Renaissance.

Perspective is more than a tool of investigation. In a painting, people, buildings and other objects could now be related to each other by scientific means. Perspective gave an integrated view of a world in which reality mattered more than ever before. This desire for an integrated view of the world, to bring all the elements which compose it together and make them dependent on each other, was also pursued by other mathematical means.

5 **6**

In Piero della Francesca's painting of the Flagellation, **1**, perspective is used to give a sense of space in which the people move and the action takes place. They are harmonised by this device. Furthermore, if you measure the distances between the two farthest roof beams and the two nearer ones and compare them you will find that they are related in the golden proportion, 1:1.618. The recession of the roof, already explained through mathematical perspective, is made more harmonious through a harmonious relationship of the parts. Since several such relationships exist in the painting, the many different parts are related and the whole becomes more easily grasped in one total vision.

This method of creating a total effect rather than merely a sum of many details was also used by architects. The palace in Rome known as the Cancellaria, **2**, **3**, designed by Bramante in 1486, consists of a number of different bays. In drawing **4** the top storey of one such bay is shown. The large window, the small window and the whole bay have the same proportions, once again the golden proportion. If we add the two smaller bays, yet another golden proportion rectangle is formed, this time lying on its side. Not only the proportion but also the relative position of each part is determined by the others. The diagonal through the large window determines the height of the base of the pilaster; the diagonal through the combined side

1

2 3

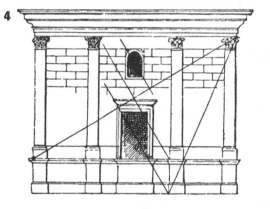

4

bay and base of pilaster determines the width of the pedestal, and so on. This means that each part gives a clue to the whole, and all the parts combine to form one total harmony.

This new way of looking at things crept into the way in which people thought of their towns. The painting by Piero della Francesca, **5**, shows how the artist thought of an ideal town in terms of a most complex system of perspective. Buildings are related to each other not only by their common visual language but also by their positioning in space. Although the scheme was not carried out at that time, the thought was there, and, as so often happens, bore fruit later.

The visual thinking which was applied to Renaissance painting, sculpture and architecture did in the end affect the face of the Renaissance town, but the influence made itself felt more slowly. Streets were still rows of individual houses, even if they were designed in the new visual language. It was in the larger civic spaces that the new attitudes reshaped the appearance of the human environment.

5

1

The earliest Renaissance building to be erected was Brunelleschi's Foundling Hospital designed in 1419 in the Piazza Annunziata in Florence, **1**, **2**. The open arcaded front of the building creates a sense of spaciousness. It is a composition in which the horizontals dominate: the cornices, the triangular pediments of the windows, even the arches seem to leap from capital to capital across the façade. Successive architects have added other buildings

2

to this square in harmony with Brunelleschi's, one of them the church from which the square takes its name. This is distinguished by nothing more than a canopy over its central arch. Obviously it had been the architects' aim to preserve the unity of the square, to see it as one space enclosed by houses, designed as such and not allowed to grow haphazardly as in a medieval town. This fact marks it as a true creation of the Renaissance. Just as Piero della Francesca and Bramante devised systems which brought all the parts of a work of art together in one easily-understood whole, so the architects of this Florentine square brought together what would normally have been individual buildings into one unified idea of a square. The open arcades allow the space to flow; they divide space without actually shutting off our view, as a wall would. They define the frontal plane of the buildings, but the space which the buildings enclose, the space of the square, is allowed to enter the structure of the buildings. We can see three entities in this square: the solid forms of the buildings, the space which forms the square, and the arcaded walk which surrounds it and which belongs to both buildings and square.

We have seen similar arrangements in medieval towns but here one feels that the architects were actively concerned with considerations of space: the thin columns make not only for greater elegance and a certain gaiety and lightheartedness, but they also allow the space to flow more freely. Giotto had thought about this many years earlier. He too painted slender columns, much thinner than were used at the time, so that the space which he tried to describe should be allowed to move freely and not be overpowered by the heavy solid forms of the pillars.

The large equestrian statue in the middle of the square is yet another expression of Renaissance visual thinking: man seen standing alone in space and not as an element of a building. And yet the monument is obviously meant to be seen, not in isolation, but in relation to the architecture. If the square is entered by the main street which links it with the cathedral, **4**, **5**, the equestrian statue is seen against the arcade of the church, which then links it visually to the two sides of the square. The two fountains are also related to the architecture: they are in line with the entrance to the Foundling Hospital. These three free-standing items, now sadly spoilt by surrounding barriers isolating them from the square, also form valuable reference points in space. A large open space is difficult to experience if we have nothing to measure against it. Pieces of sculpture, such as these, help us to take in the recession of the space; they act as visual stepping stones across an unknown expanse.

3

4

5

6

7   **8**

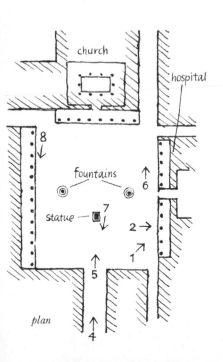

church

hospital

8

fountains

6

statue   7

2

1

5

4

plan

35

St. Mark's Square in Venice is an even more refined expression of the Renaissance realisation of space in town design. It is an irregular space, made even more irregular by the addition of a smaller square, the Piazzetta, which connects it with the sea front, **1**. Both squares form one large space which is surrounded by buildings and arcades designed to give a unified, but not uniform, appearance. The buildings are variations on a theme and so form a pattern which conforms to the principle of variety within unity—an ideal artists have always tried to achieve.

We can approach St. Mark's Square from a number of different access points, which are, however, hidden by the arcade which skirts the square. We may come from a shopping street, **2**, or a residential square, **3**, and pass through a typical opening, such as **4**, which occurs at the end farthest away from the basilica. We enter through an archway, and through a vaulted thoroughfare reach the arcade, **5**. Left and right the arcade extends to the corners of the square, and from them to the far end are a covered walk and shopping precinct. On passing into the vast square, the first building to attract our attention is the basilica of St. Mark, with its gleaming cupolas, **6**. To the right stands the clocktower. Through the gap between this and the building on the extreme right the Gothic Ducal Palace is visible. To the left of the basilica the space recedes, first into a

1

2

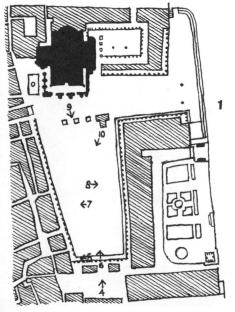

3

4

6

5

small court, then into a narrow street. We can see now that we are standing in a space which is closed on three sides. The basilica shuts off the fourth side, but allows the space to flow to the left in line with our view into the court, to the right in line with its façade. In this horizontal composition the belltower acts as the only vertical relief, as a visual rallying point. As we walk across the Piazza towards the basilica we notice that the two façades facing each other left and right are dissimilar, yet harmonise, **7**, **8**. From the front of the basilica we look to the point where we entered the square. Now we see that the buildings forming the two long sides of the square are of unequal height, but are related to each other by the far building, **9**, which has two items in common with each of its neighbours: the skyline and one cornice with the Old Town Hall (right) and two cornices with the New Town Hall (left). Furthermore, one element (the upper cornice) is common to all three buildings. In this way two dissimilar sides of the Piazza are brought into harmony by the third. We also notice that the square seems much longer in this direction than it seemed when viewed against the basilica. Seen in this direction it has a strange, spacious quality; the patterned floor recedes in a most dramatic manner and the far end seems very far away. This phenomenon is the result of a deliberate tampering with the laws of perspective. As you can see from the top of the free-standing belltower, **10**, the Piazza is not really rectangular, its two sides taper away from the basilica. This has the effect of 'speeding up' or 'slowing down' the recession, depending on the direction in which you look, so that the space is never the same. This adds not only an element of visual surprise to our experience of the Piazza as a space, but also a feeling of movement.

7

8

9

10

From the court next to the basilica we can get an even more surprising perspective view of the square, **1**, although we cannot see both the long sides. As we pass in front of the basilica the view of the square keeps changing. We now experience the open space in relation to the tower. We can look down the square to the right of the tower and see the tower in relation to the Old Town Hall, **2**, or in relation to the ornate and serene Library, and experience the perspective between them, **3**, or we can see the tower in relation to the whole square and feel the space flowing right round it, **4**. As we walk away from the basilica we can see the farthest corner of the square through the gap between tower and Library, **5**. The number of surprising views is unlimited.

We are now in the Piazzetta. This was the traditional link between the main square and the sea, the approach route of visiting merchants from the landing stage. Between the two columns at the far end of the Piazzetta we see Palladio's famous Church of the Redeemer standing on an island at the mouth of the Grand Canal, **6**. The two columns provide a visual barrier and stop the view of the Piazzetta from running right into the sea. This can be better appreciated from the top of the tower, **8**, from which we can also get an idea of the relationship between Piazzetta, Ducal Palace and landing stage; the heart of Venice is thus open to the sea without being completely exposed to it, **9**. From the end of the Piazzetta we look back before turning onto the quay, **7**, **10**, **11**. From the

1

2

4

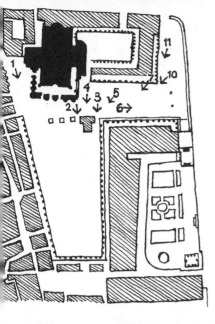

7

8 9

10 11

1

2

wide arcades of the Ducal Palace we can still see
diagonally across the length of the Piazzetta and
the breadth of the Piazza, a long view. From
farther along the quay we see the Library
jutting out beyond the level of the Ducal Palace, **1**.
This is the view we would have obtained had we
approached St. Mark's Square from the landing
stage: a magnificent invitation to enter. The
free-standing column marks the outpost of the inner
civic space. The façade of the Ducal Palace on the
right leads the eye to Sansovino's Library,
which, with a graceful gesture, deflects it to the
right. On the left and in the distance, across the
Grand Canal, the church of Santa Maria della
Salute rises into sight.

A walk through this complex civic space is so
delightful not only on account of the spatial
relationships we experience, but also from several

other points of view. One of these is that the
character of the space in which we move keeps
changing, so that no sameness and dullness are
experienced. Consider again the different enclosures
we have passed through on our brief tour: a
narrow side street; a dark mysterious enclosure
of vaults as we passed under the building; the
sudden shock we received as we emerged from it
and entered the large Piazza, as we passed from a
small intimate enclosure into a wide and formal
one; the small court, which links the large civic
space with the more intimate ones of the smaller
thoroughfares; the Piazzetta which has only two
built-up sides, with the clearly defined space of
the Piazza at one end and the openness of the quay
at the other; finally the quay itself, half townscape,
half seascape. At each stage, as we pass from one
kind of space to another, there are articulations
which help us—unconsciously—to distinguish them:
the arcade, the three flagpoles in front of the
basilica, the two columns at the end of the
Piazzetta; all these are punctuation marks in the
complete spatial sentence. The huge tower stands
at the turning-point of the whole complex, the
kingpin upon which it all revolves. Its visual
prominence is therefore justified. The whole is a
magnificent visual statement. Add to this the lesser
items which give it its character and flavour, such
as the architectural details and ornaments, and
even the pigeons without which the square is
unthinkable, and you have perhaps the most
significant and delightful civic space ever contrived.
But since Venice's fall from power it survives only
as a museum piece.

The Piazza Campidoglio on the Capitoline Hill in Rome was first projected by Michelangelo in 1538 but more than a century had to elapse before its full realisation. In spite of the passage of time and the different architects to whom it fell to translate Michelangelo's ideas into reality, the original plan changed but little and what we see today is in essence very much what Michelangelo wanted. Very little of the piazza and its buildings is visible as we begin our ascent of the long ramp, **3**. Gradually, as we climb, the central building rises into our field of vision, **4**, but we do not see the full extent of the piazza until we reach the very top of the ramp, **5**.

Although we are not immediately aware of it, the two side buildings are not parallel to each other, so that we enter the piazza at its narrowest side. The perspective effect of this arrangement brings the main building forward; coming on top of the apparent movement of the building as we approached the piazza, this creates a unique sensation of space and makes the piazza seem larger than it is. Unlike earlier Renaissance piazzas, this one is not enclosed; there is only a visual barrier at its fourth (open) side. The space can flow to and fro, aided by the magnificent view of Rome which is framed by the architecture of the piazza.

4

5

7

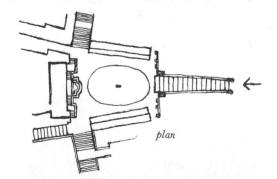

plan

*The equestrian statue of the emperor Marcus Aurelius stands in the middle of the oval. It forms a foil to the architecture of the central building, **6**, and of the side buildings, **7**. Note the classical figures on the roof line.*

As we investigate, it becomes obvious that here a great sculptor has been at work. The many different levels are linked by stairs which allow one to experience this complex as one large piece of sculpture, in three dimensions. They are so designed that the view from any point, at any level, should link one's own viewpoint to the rest of the piazza. Some of the changes in level are extremely subtle; for instance the central oval is slightly lower than the ground on which the buildings stand, but towards the monument it rises again.

All this seems to have only one purpose: a modelling of space, such as only one of the greatest sculptors that ever lived could have attained. Civic design had reached perfection.

1

2   3

4   5

6

7

8

The sensation of space is
increased by the slightly
convex surface of the oval
which can be seen in **7**, and
the floor pattern, **1**, **2**, which
leads one to walk round the
central space rather than across
it. Being an essentially
sculpturesque, three-
dimensional design the
changing sunlight has a
marked effect on it. As the day
wears on the many varied
facets of this miraculous work,
4 and **5**, **6** and **8**, reveal
themselves. The differences in
the observer's level likewise
produce an ever-changing
succession of views and
sensations of space
and form, **8**, **9**.
The piazza is a complicated
and rich work of art whose
true character unfolds itself
slowly as we explore it. It is
the work of a master mind—
every detail, **3**, contains the
perfection of the whole.

9

1

2

The visual language of the Renaissance was an
Italian product. It corresponded to many values and
conditions which were typically Italian and for
which at the time an equivalent hardly existed
elsewhere. Eventually it was to prove decisive in
forming the visual language of the whole of Europe;
but although it spread northwards from Italy and
was eagerly taken up by artists, architects and
designers, it was not properly understood for a long
time. It also had considerable opposition from
craftsmen who worked in the local tradition and to
whom the new visual language was a foreign idiom.
The painting of the Adoration in Cologne
cathedral, **1**, was painted about the middle of the
15th century. It is most meticulously painted. The
patterns of the drapery and each single fold are
accurately recorded; obviously a great deal of
observation of everyday life went into this charming
painting. But the space in which the action of the
painting takes place is not defined at all, as though
the artist had not been conscious of its existence.
There is no background which might connect the
scene with the real world. In a way this painting
reminds one of the sculpture on the pulpit in Siena
cathedral. In spite of the wealth of naturalistic
detail the picture is still closer to the medieval
world than to that which the Renaissance had just
opened up.

3

Buildings too remained faithful to the old medieval traditions, although Renaissance decorations became an ever more important part of their outward appearance. The façade (1590) of an old house in Brunswick, **2**, bears Renaissance motifs but they are applied with less skill and assurance than those on an Italian building and their proportions are not so refined. The stone balusters of the first floor balcony however are still in the Gothic tradition. The high gable likewise gives it an unmistakable northern Gothic character.

The same story was repeated in most European countries, but nowhere did such an authoritative adaptation of the Renaissance occur as in France. The structure of buildings, often designed by imported Italian architects, bore unmistakable signs of the Renaissance, but details and decorations were still in the old medieval idiom. The Chateau de Chambord built in 1519, **3**, is an example. It expresses the new Renaissance elements of architecture through its symmetry and horizontality; but its round turrets, a left-over idea from the days of the feudal castle, high roof with countless tall chimneys, dormer windows, and spires give it a distinct Gothic appearance. However, by the middle of the sixteenth century French architects had become sufficiently acquainted with these new visual ideas to handle them in a typically French way.

The Renaissance façade of the Louvre, built by Lescot in 1546, **4**, shows that French architects had reached a point where they could go beyond copying decorative details and had learned to express themselves in the new visual language. The niches between paired columns are a typically French motif. The high roof shows that this palace was built north of the Alps and the windows, arranged in vertical rows rather than in horizontal rows as in an Italian palace, again betray northern modes of thought.

4

1

2

In England, the medieval language was still evident
in the sixteenth century. Little Moreton Hall, **1**,
built in 1550 one hundred and twenty-five years
after San Lorenzo, is a rambling, picturesque,
conglomeration of small units, and its interior shows
how much use was made of local materials by local
craftsmen, **2**.

Such buildings must have made sense to the people
of the time whereas the newly-imported Renaissance
ideas, which were quite unrelated to their way of
thinking and feeling did not. Yet here and there
ornaments in the Renaissance idiom began to
appear because artists and craftsmen from the
continent, invited to work in England, added their
ornaments to buildings conceived in the medieval
visual language. The hammerbeam roof of the
Great Hall at Hampton Court is still a medieval
structure and the Renaissance ornaments carved on
its members could not be more out of place.

When Henry VIII broke with Rome direct Italian
influence became very much weaker and further
Renaissance impulses reached England chiefly
through France and Holland. At Burleigh House
(1585), **3**, these influences can be easily seen. The
columns and arches are of the Renaissance, but
French not Italian Renaissance, as a comparison
with Lescot's Louvre façade will show. The
fretwork-like ornament on the top story is of Dutch
origin. The obelisks and high roof give it a northern
look. The mullioned bay windows of the second

3

4

5

floor are typically English; so are the paired
chimneys, but they are made to resemble Italian
columns. At Longleat House (1572) these foreign
influences were kept at bay and a more genuinely
English interpretation of the Renaissance begins to
emerge, **4**. The house has a true Renaissance
entrance porch. The Dutch ornaments on the roof
line are used with restraint and discretion. The
house has a strong horizontal emphasis, both as a
result of its overall proportions and the many
horizontal lines: cornices, balusters, string courses.
But the protrusions caused by the bay windows
produce a vertical element in the design which is
stressed by the emphatically upright windows and
chimney stacks. These two emphases—vertical and
horizontal—are in perfect balance, neither is allowed
to suppress the other. The general appearance of
the house is rather grid-like.

But smaller houses hardly took part in this evolution.
As towns grew and larger houses became necessary
to provide dwellings for their increasing populations,
medieval methods were still followed. In this
picture, **5**, we can see that even as late as the
seventeenth century houses in London (and other
English towns) had hardly changed since medieval
times. The distorted carvings, ill-fitting Renaissance
decorations on a now incongruous jettied structure,
show that the Renaissance spirit and the
Renaissance use of space were late to make their
mark on the English town.

1

During the sixteenth century an element of
discord could be discerned in the visual arts.
We have seen that the Renaissance had created
a consciousness of space as a means to establish a
new visual reality, harmonious and balanced.
But now paintings could be seen in which this
deep understanding of spatial relationships was no
longer evident. This tendency is referred to as
Mannerism. In the painting entitled Joseph in
Egypt, by Pontormo, **1**, painted in 1519, it is more
difficult than in earlier Renaissance paintings to
understand the space in which the people move and
exist. The curved staircase on the right is ambiguous.
The staircase in the foreground is difficult to
relate to the other parts of the picture because we
cannot see its farthest edge. The group of people
in the middle distance does not link up with the

rest. The space of the picture is hardly defined at
all. Several figures are out of scale, so that even
relationships of scale are eliminated. It is as though
the artist had striven *against* all those principles
which the artists of the Renaissance had worked so
hard to establish. Parmigianino's Madonna, **2**,
painted in 1532, shows similar inconsistencies. The
figures are crowded into an ill-defined space; the
position in space of the small figure on the right is
doubtful, he also seems to be out of scale. The
figures, including the child, have been subjected
to an excessive elongation, no doubt to give an
impression of elegance, which is emphasised by the
tall column in the background. The Renaissance
artist had attempted to portray a balanced vision,
but now the very opposite seems to be the aim:
instability, tension.

We might say that this trend was due to the fact that these artists of the sixteenth century must have felt that all the great things had been achieved by their predecessors, the giants of the Italian Renaissance: Titian, Leonardo, Raphael. It was impossible to improve on the works of these great artists, and their successors became self-conscious in their attempts to progress from this high peak in artistic creation. Distortion, ambiguity took the place of reason and balance, cleverness and elegance were at a premium.

Deeper reasons for this change suggest themselves. After the optimism of the Renaissance a wave of insecurity swept across Italy. The Reformation cast doubts on the constituted order of Christianity. Italy became a battlefield, Rome was sacked in 1527, many of its inhabitants fell victim to murder and rape, many houses were destroyed, and the Vatican turned into a barracks. Florence suffered a similar fate three years later. Foreign domination asserted itself, often through local rulers, and the Pope himself entered into financial and political deals with the foreign oppressors. A series of financial crises must have left its mark not only on the minds of all those merchants and craftsmen who were affected by them, but also on others who imagined that they too might become involved. The social, religious and political insecurity, even a feeling of impending doom, is conveyed by the art of the period with greater precision and power than in the writings of historians. The restlessness, the tension, the turmoil, the lack of logic and of harmony, and the elegance and sophistication which cloak them, are an accurate mirror of the mental climate of the period.

Naturally this attitude was not confined to painting; it affected the face of towns in many ways. The Uffizi in Florence, **3**, were designed by Vasari in 1560 as the ducal offices. A needlessly heavy cornice runs along the front of the two wings which face each other. Brackets below small platforms where the cornice broadens out support nothing at all. Every detail appears to have been designed for effect, rather than from an understanding of the natural harmony of parts. The two wings enclose an unnaturally narrow space considering the height of the building, which is also excessively long and uniform in effect. The harmony between the height of the buildings and the breadth and width of the space they enclose, which a true Renaissance architect would have built into a scheme of this nature, is absent. Instead we experience an irresistible sense of perspective, as though we were going to be drawn relentlessly through a narrow tube, and quite different from the gentle perspective effect of St. Mark's Square. Perspective has now become more important than space, the tool more important than the purpose

2

3

1 *Another view of the Uffizi*

for which it was created. A similar effect can be observed in Parmigianino's painting, where the recession between the foreground and the standing figure in the background is exaggerated and overstressed, while the space itself is uncertain. At the far end of the Uffizi is the large civic square in front of the town hall. At the corner of the town hall is a fountain, designed by Ammanati in 1571. One of the figures from this fountain is shown in picture **2**. It is, like Parmigianino's Madonna, excessively elongated in an attempt to obtain greater elegance. The actual positioning of the figure is doubtful and uneasy, as though it might slip off its uncomfortable perch. It makes us feel on edge. Obviously the artist who sculptured this figure had different aims from, say, Donatello, as much as Vasari had different aims from Brunelleschi or Bramante. Elegance and tension had become the most sought-after effects, and took the place of harmony and balance.
The Renaissance was over.

2

3   The Baroque town

The conditions which gave rise to the uncertainty of Mannerism began to consolidate. Rome as the seat of the papacy once more rose to its former importance and in some ways exceeded it. For now the counter-reformation made it the centre of the religious conflict which rent the western world. In this conflict the greatest artistic talent Italy could muster was thrown into the battle. During the Middle Ages the Catholic Church had been the undisputed repository of Christianity. But now its position was threatened. New ideas challenged the old-established beliefs; those whom the church looked on as heretics enticed away the devotion of the faithful. The Catholic Church could regain its former hold over the people only by a strong appeal to their emotions—a much more effective means than rational argument. The Gothic cathedral had been able to afford to be delicate and ethereal, it had sung a song of praise to God and the saints and, by the magnificence of its song, had induced people to sing with it. But the assignment of the Baroque church was much tougher. It needed to impress, to invite, more than that, it needed to be militant in the face of opposition. Size is obviously one way to impress people, but whereas the Gothic church could soar, the Baroque church had to be impressive in a worldly way, for it had to compete not only with the new alternative forms of Christianity but also with the richly massive houses and palaces around it, the symbols of material wealth.

When we look at the interior of St. Peter's in Rome, 1, we see the meaning of this demonstrated. The space within the church is so enormous, the masses of stone which contain it of such unbelievably gigantic dimensions, that the individual is made to

1

1

feel very small indeed. This is the expression of militant Christianity; we are made aware not only of the splendour of Christianity but also of its power. When in the Middle Ages saints were depicted, their spiritual rather than their physical qualities were emphasised; now they began to be shown as well-made, handsome human beings with a physical presence somewhat larger than life, **1**. The church itself made the most of its riches and power and displayed them in the most effective manner.

This movement led to a concept of space which was as different from that of the preceding eras as the mental climate which produced it. It can best be understood by studying the plans which Bramante and Michelangelo devised for St. Peter's. Bramante's plan, **2**, which he prepared in 1506 is still in the Renaissance visual language: a number of interrelated spaces, which are partly independent and partly belong to a larger whole. Each room of this design can be seen and experienced in its own right, as well as a part of the overall pattern. It is the expression of the Renaissance idea of harmony. Michelangelo's design of 1546, **3**, differs in its main conception: here we have a composition comprising far fewer individual rooms linked in a direct way to form a large complex space, rather than a series of smaller ones. Although each one of the smaller rooms can be seen as a subdivision of the larger one, they have no existence in their own right, as in Bramante's design. Everything is sacrificed to the main idea of a central space. Massiveness and centralisation then emerge as the dominant features of the Baroque. Rows of superimposed columns or pilasters as we see them in Renaissance architecture are now abandoned in favour of giant pilasters which span several floors, thereby increasing the sense of scale, **4**.

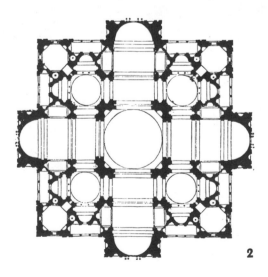

2

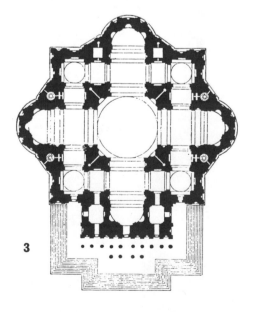

3

4 *St. Peter's, Rome*
5, 6 *The colonnade in front of St Peter's. Note the size of the human figure*

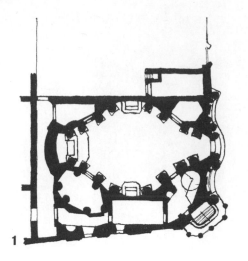

1

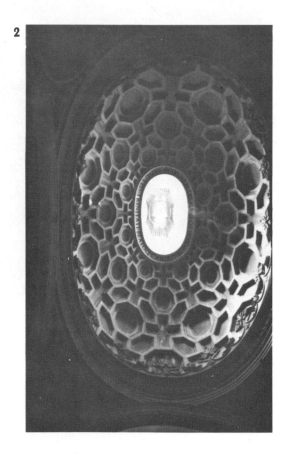

2 *The cupola*

The idea of the large unified space is also expressed in smaller Baroque churches. Picture **1** shows the plan of the church San Carlo alle Quatro Fontane designed by Borromini, perhaps the most original of all Baroque architects, in 1633. The cruciform church plan of earlier periods has been changed: the four arms of the cross are still there but in a somewhat mitigated form, as though the cruciform shape had been molten and allowed to re-form itself under different conditions. The different conditions were the new mental climate which made the architect see the whole interior of the church as *one* large space; the usual divisions into different walls are eliminated and we see what amounts to *one* large wall billowing round the enclosed space. The exterior of the church, **3**, extends this idea. The façade, which in no way reflects the structure of the interior, has a series of hollows so that cornices instead of moving along in straight lines, describe rhythmic figures surging forward and backward, **5**. But there are also shapes which run in opposition to this rhythm, for instance the balcony-like structure on the first floor, and the steps. They create rhythms which run against the main one, and so create a certain tension. The Renaissance wall was always flat, but now the wall recedes and advances in turns and seems to make an emotional appeal to us. What is more, the counter-movement of balcony and stairs both enriches this appeal and creates a tension, rather like that of simultaneous rhythms in music or of two melodies heard at the same time, which at times harmonise and at other times contradict each other. The music of this period did in fact often contain two or more melodies played at the same time. This device is referred to as *counterpoint* and we can call the architectural device which it resembles *visual counterpoint*. We shall find it again and again in Baroque architecture.

Baroque artists attempted to bring about an integration even more thorough than was ever attempted during the Renaissance, that is to say, a state of affairs in which every element has its allotted part to play in the interest of the total effect. Architects had to relate their buildings to their environments and this they did in many ingenious ways. For instance the sculptured panel with its fountain on the left of the façade of San Carlo has its counterpart on each of the other three corners of the crossroads on which the church stands, **4**, **6**. In this way the church has been integrated with its surrounding buildings and takes its place in the larger scheme of the townscape. This particular spot is especially favoured: the crossroads is on a hill from which the roads can be seen receding into the distance in an impressive perspective view. As we shall see, perspective was of particular significance to the Baroque mind.

3 **4**

5 **6**

Picture **1** shows another example of the integration of Baroque buildings with the existing townscape. A Baroque church, also by Borromini, with its curved façade, contrasts with the flat façade of the earlier Renaissance church next to it. But the architecture has been related to the older church and the central cornice runs right across the combined façades.

2, 3 *Baroque harmony between buildings and street furniture*

1

2

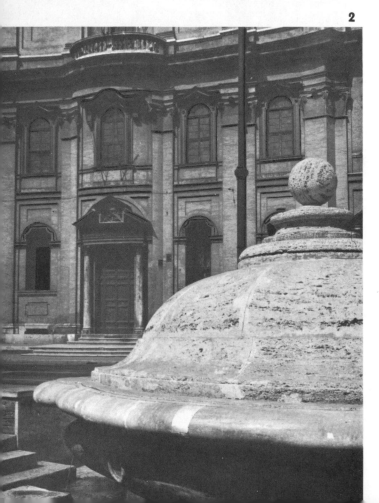

3

One of the most interesting buildings by Borromini is the small church of St. Ivo in Rome, **4**. It is built between two older buildings and again shows how a master architect can find complete expression for his own ideas and at the same time fit in with those of an earlier period. From the outside we are conscious once more of successive convex and concave curves: visual counterpoint, **5**. The interior is characterised by a high cupola of great geometric complexity, **6**. Photographs, which after all are printed on a flat surface, cannot possibly do justice to this structure, which is so eminently three-dimensional, and can come into its own only when experienced in three dimensions by an observer, who can move about so that all the relationships are given scope to change

and develop. Architecture is here very close to sculpture. With its richly decorated surfaces, this cupola gives a unique sensation of form and space. The curvatures have been compared to those of sails in the wind. Although Borromini's inventions rival the grace of sails blown by the wind, even a casual glance will reveal that his inspiration was not only sensuous but also intellectual. He must have had a very good grasp of geometrical principles to design this structure. Science had advanced since the days of the Renaissance and had become even more mathematical and precise; it influenced the way people thought and felt in every sphere. The Baroque, by combining emotional and intellectual elements, mystical and scientific ideas, brought about the union of two divergent sides of human nature.

4
5

6

1

2

The emotional climate of much of the Baroque period led artists to explore several new methods of expression. To give a painting or a piece of sculpture an emotional impact its dramatic side must be stressed. Gestures become more eloquent, facial expressions exaggerated, movement violent. In a painting the lighting is arranged to make the most of the already dramatic situation. In sculpture the forms and surfaces are shaped to catch as much varied light as possible, for the same reason. This example, **1**, comes from the façade of the church of Santa Maria della Salute in Venice, begun in 1632, and we can see that the same principle holds good for the rest of the façade, **2**, which is broken up into many small facets to catch the light. Never before had lighting effects been used in this way, which explains why Baroque architecture and sculpture look best in strong sunlight: they were designed for it.

Picture **4** shows the ceiling painting in the church of St. Ignatius in Rome. It demonstrates the points we have already discussed. It also shows that the artist was much concerned with the problem of recession into space, to such an extent that the shape of the ceiling—a barrel vault—is disguised, and the illusion of a new architectural shape is created by a most skilful use of perspective.

It is difficult to decide which part of the architecture is real and which is painted—it is equally difficult to tell the difference between painted and sculpted figures and ornaments. This extreme use of perspective is quite different from the still more exaggerated but purposeless Mannerist perspective. Here it has a dual purpose: to create the idea of infinity so beloved of the Baroque mind because it expressed religious and philosophical concepts of the time, the mystical infinity of God, the infinity of space as explored by mathematics, and to integrate painting with architecture. The integration of painting with *sculpture* is brought about by the strong light and shade effects. This total integration of three arts is however based on illusion. The preoccupation with perspective as a means of illusion had its architectural counterpart in such buildings as the Palazzo Barberini in Rome, **3**, where the top floor windows, although almost flat, appear to recede into the wall.

3

The townscape, as we have noted before, is slow to reflect all the new tendencies of an age. It is not often that a whole square or street is completely rebuilt; usually the town designer has to accept what the past has handed to him and fit the new ideas of his age into an existing pattern. But although the number of his additions may be few, they may be important enough to give the whole environment a new character, a contemporary look. The Piazza Navona in Rome, **1**, is a civic space— it can hardly be called a square—which derives its unusual shape from the Roman arena which once occupied this site. It was already in use as a civic space when the Baroque designers got to work on it. They did not redesign it completely but instead added buildings, sculpture and fountains which gave it a distinctly Baroque appearance.

The centrepiece is clearly the church of St. Agnes, **5**, designed by Rainaldi, with a façade designed by Borromini. It has all the usual Baroque features, with which we are now familiar: curved walls, visual counterpoint, ornaments and deep recesses to increase the variety of light and so to dramatise the whole elevation. But it is quite definitely designed with regard to the square: it has a central position, its wings outspread and advancing as if to embrace the square and everyone in it, **3**. Furthermore, the cupola is set well forward so that it can be admired from almost any point in the square. At St. Peter's the cupola is set back, with the result that even from the very large space in front of the cathedral it cannot be seen in its entirety. In a narrow space such as the Piazza Navona it was even more important to place the cupola forward if it was to play its part in the general effect of the piazza.

There are three fountains in the piazza, two smaller ones at either end and a large one in the middle. Actually the large fountain, the Fountain of the Four Rivers, by Bernini, is not *quite* in the middle. Like an obsequious servant it concedes the central position to the church of St. Agnes. The smaller fountains not only complete the scheme but prepare us, as we enter the piazza, **2**, for the larger spectacle that awaits us in the centre. These sculptural fountains speak the same language as the church. Bernini's is the most developed of the three, **6**. The play of light, the heavy, ponderous masses in movement, the exaggerated gestures, the ornateness, all these are Baroque features, which relate it to the church. The deep recesses even succeed in penetrating the full depth of the form, both in the fountain, and in the towers of the church, **8**. Their common visual language ties the pagan fountains to the Christian church. Without this exciting Baroque focus the piazza would have had a nondescript appearance. The skill of the Baroque designers gave it a visual cohesion, to match its social cohesion. For this is in the truest sense of the word a *civic* space; it is used by the inhabitants as a social meeting place, by the children as a safe playground, **4**. Up to the eighteenth century it was also used for festivities and as a market place. It is one of the happiest of Baroque town designs, where the human scale is not suppressed, as in the larger Baroque schemes, but enhanced and illuminated by the splendour of art.

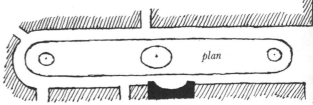

plan

1   2

3

4

5

6

7

8

1 *A windmill which works two sets of millstones at the same time. The beginning of mass production is in sight.*

1

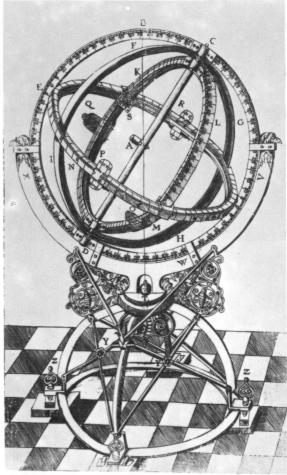

2

As the Baroque era progressed, science and technology made great advances. Machines, invented to make large scale production possible, were becoming more and more complex. As picture **1** shows, they were no longer the rather crude devices of medieval or even Renaissance engineers, but much subtler and more efficient, so that John Carey could write in 1695 'Cranes and blocks help to draw up more for one shilling than men's labour without them would do for five'. Scientists were now able to describe and calculate complicated movements and curvatures. Newton invented the calculus, by which curvatures, such as the vaults of Baroque churches, could be calculated. Galileo shed new light on the structure of the solar system. Models of it were now produced showing ever-growing complexity of inter-dependent movements. Similar tendencies are evident in instruments of that date, in which many diverse movements are related, **2**. These complicated movements took place in three dimensions, not in two, as, for example, the movement in a simple pulley.

While Renaissance thinkers had begun to explore space by discovering and examining spatial relationships, it was only now that man was able to conceive of complex movements in three-dimensional space, such as we can see in nature. It was only now that mathematical and scientific advances gave him the means of investigating not only spatial dimensions but also the movement through which alone they can be experienced. Architects and artists began to think more and more in terms of three-dimensional movement. This tendency was most evident in the design of staircases.

During medieval times the staircase was no more than a necessary evil. The medieval newel staircase shown in **3** leads to the upper floor of the Jewel Tower in London. It is rather like a tunnel through the masonry. There is little thought of traversing space in its construction; the user can see only a small part of his path at any one time. The Renaissance, with its new realisation of space, introduced more open structures by straightening out the stairs, **4**, and eventually opening up a stairwell. The space through which the user of the staircase moved could now be seen and felt. The Baroque period took this development one significant step further. Not only did Baroque architects build elaborate staircases at the slightest provocation, **5**, but these became more complex in a spatial sense, twisting in spirals and complicated curves, going round corners, following the structure of the building or cutting across it, as through the architect had attempted to explore the space enclosed by the building and wanted us to share his experience. In fact, staircases became the most important part of buildings and occupied a disproportionately large space. A great deal of thought was spent on their design.

4 *The staircase of the Ducal Palace, Urbino, Italy, and* **5** *of the Palazzo Madama, Turin.*

3

4

5

1

This mania for staircases of a complex, three-dimensional nature soon affected the outside of buildings as well, as in this example, **1**, of the church of SS. Domenico and Sisto, in Rome. In the end it even affected the appearance of the town by the construction of flights of steps in civic spaces. The Spanish Steps in Rome, **2**, are the most impressive example of this. Here we have a combination of many movements, intertwining, parting, running in counterpoint, re-uniting, in a carefully composed set-piece of spatial exploration. Superficially it appears to be a free and exuberant pattern, and we can take one of several possible routes in ascending the staircase, but this freedom is only apparent and illusory; it takes place in a strictly limited compass of symmetry on either side of a fixed axis, and in the end, whichever route we choose, we must end up at the church doors. The Baroque does in fact, in spite of an illusion of freedom, control movement in a way which was unknown in earlier periods.

2 **3**

4

5   **6**

7   **8**

9

Less easily comprehensible and more dynamic than Michelangelo's Piazza Campidoglio, the Spanish Steps have movement—complicated, concerted movement—as their main theme. Seen from the top landing, the lower landing with its billowing balustrade and fine baroque perspective view complete the sensation of movement, **8**, *whose symmetry and counterpoint are somewhat reminiscent of certain scientific and technological devices of the day, such as the distillery,* **6**.

Fundamental changes in ways of thinking, which, as we have seen, often result in the formation of a new visual language, are always an amalgamation of many widely-spread, often conflicting and contradictory ideas. We have already mentioned a number of such ideas which contributed to the Baroque visual language, and we shall discover more and more the further we investigate the mental climate in which it grew. The curving wall, with its suggestion of movement, had overtones which fitted the demands of the new Catholicism, through which the church was re-asserting its authority. The grand scale of buildings stressed the idea of authority, often of secular authority. Now that new kingdoms were arising, and political authority was becoming more centralised, the idea of a capital city as the seat of the ruler and the splendour of courtly life became more potent in shaping the face of the town. A magnificent building will grow in stature if it is sited so that the people's gaze is directed towards it; two churches will act as a visual magnet where one might not, **3**. The medieval town was a series of human habitations, the street so many houses placed in a row. The Renaissance brought greater unity and a spatial conception to this basic layout. The Baroque added movement. The street was no longer seen primarily as a sum of human cells, but as a track along which movement may take place. Again we must look to Rome for the earliest examples of this, to Rome, where Pope Sixtus V did much reconstruction work and where many of the most creative schemes are due to his efforts.

1

2

In picture **1** you see a part of Rome as it existed before Pope Sixtus V took office. Streets rambled and meandered because they were not laid out in order to get the traveller from one point to another, but rather as houses happened to be built, or to follow a favourite footpath which may have existed before this particular piece of land was built on. In the reconstruction of Rome the new streets did not follow the routes of the earlier ones. The idea of movement had entered into town planning, streets were made in order to get from one point to another and since the shortest connection between any two points is the straight line, streets became increasingly rectilinear, **2**. Often they converged and formed star-like patterns, which in turn connected with other such junctions. All this had a unifying effect on the face of the Baroque town. Because streets were considered by Baroque town planners as channels for movement, junctions and intersections of streets assumed a new importance. Movement, in the Baroque sense, is never free; it must be disciplined to follow the tracks laid down by authority. At junctions and intersections of streets authority must therefore make a showing, for it is there that the movement is changed and re-directed into different channels.

3 *Piazza San Carlo, Turin*

4

5

The Piazza del Popolo is really a road junction. As the plan, **7**, shows, the city entered at one end of the piazza, while at the other end three roads lead to different districts, the central one right into the heart of Rome. The piazza is organised to speed the movement of people and vehicles coming into the city and this organisation is expressed visually. The sequence of pictures, **4**, **5**, **6**, **8**, shows what we see as we approach the triumphal arch which marks the city boundary, and pass through it into the space beyond. The central obelisk arrests our movement, the two identical, symmetrical churches define the points where the movement must split up. The central road, between the two churches, is, by implication, the most important one. A Renaissance square is a visual statement about space, a Baroque square, more often than not, a statement about movement. The Piazza del Popolo is a receptacle for movement entering through the arch; it then disperses it to different parts of Rome. It is designed to do this efficiently and it expresses its function visually; it is, in fact, a visual command in keeping with its function. We are made conscious of control and of authority.

6

7

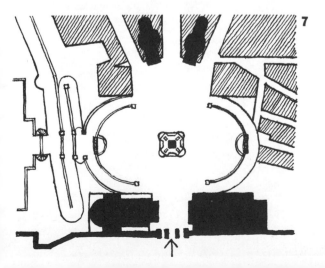

8

Although the Baroque movement began as a form of philosophical and religious expression, in harmony with the aspirations of the Roman Catholic church, it fitted so well into the planning of autocratic Europe that it became a widespread visual language. Streets which facilitated movement were important to the new rulers because they were parade grounds on which processions could take place. Such processions are important to any autocratic ruler because in this way he can impress the people with his pomp and sumptuousness, or with his military power. Narrow, winding streets were considered a threat to autocratic government since they made military protection very difficult in times of trouble. Long, straight, wide streets facilitated the movements of troops. In addition, the autocratic ruler had to be at the centre of things and his palace had to be the visual focus of the town. The court of Versailles, built 1676-88, became the ideal to be aimed at. Picture **1** shows that the whole of the town was planned to stress the importance of the court, all the main streets radiated from it and the houses curved round it. The court was the hub, as in past ages the church had been. Looking in the other direction, **2**, away from the town, we see long, trim avenues leading into the open country. From this direction too the palace was the focus. It dominated the world of man and the world of nature. The monarch was omnipotent. Such grandiose planning, was made possible by technological progress. The water works of Versailles, **3**, which was the pride of the age, made it possible for such a large building, with its many needs for domestic water, to be placed in a spot where no natural water supplies were available. This court became the model for those of other rulers, large and small. Karlsruhe, **4**, the seat of a German principality, was planned as a small version of Versailles. The prince's court had the dominant position. Without it the town would have had no purpose, for it existed solely as an adornment of the court. This modern aerial photograph shows the original planning still largely intact.

1

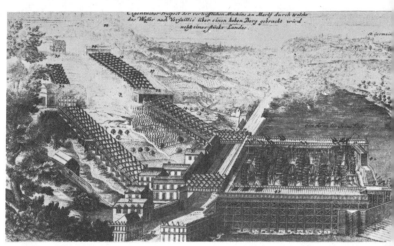

3

Baroque ideas did not die out with the period which bears this name. Emphasis on the intersection of roads as a place where authority is expressed can be found in the nineteenth century and even at the beginning of the twentieth. The Etoile in Paris, **1**, is one such example. The triumphal arch serves as a symbol of absolute power, in the absence of a palace. Another legacy from the Baroque way of thinking and building is the use of the façade to unify a street and to encourage movement through it. In time the façade, not the inside, became the important aspect of the house. Often it merely served to keep a large, unplanned heap of rubble at bay, **2**. The street was no longer a conglomeration of human dwellings, but a traffic artery.

The Rococo (the later stage of the Baroque) was nevertheless capable of providing humane townscapes, as these pictures of Nancy in France amply prove. Here the human scale seems to have been the yardstick of a whole complex, constructed for a community yet accessible to individual people. The three open spaces are conceived as a sequence and their varying characters, which add up to one unified whole, can be fully experienced only by passing from one into the other. **3**. The scheme contains a number of different types of shops and dwellings, to allow for different uses and needs. Everywhere the human scale is evident, in the sculpture and in the doors and windows of the houses which line the open space. Materials are used in a humble way; there is little in this scheme which strikes one as inflated or over-sumptuous. Elegance is its main theme. It can be seen in the curvature of the colonnade, the graceful sculptured figures marking significant spots and devoid of the often violent movement which is characteristic of Baroque sculpture. It can be seen too in the delicate wrought iron screens and gates surrounding the square without actually shutting it off from the rest of the town.

1

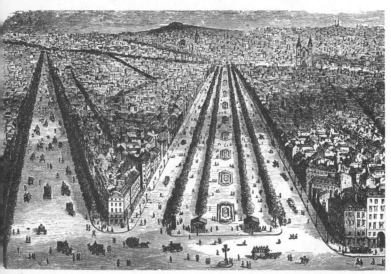

2

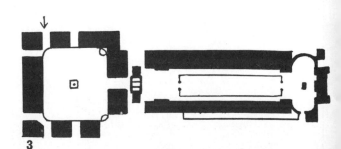

3

4　　**5**

7

6

Place Stanislas, the large square
in the plan, is formed by massive
administrative buildings and
smaller ones containing shops. It is
normally entered through one of the
delicate, wrought iron gates, **4**,
which set it apart from the rest of
the town. These decorative screens
define the space of the square; they
also link and unify buildings of
different height and function, **7**.
The Neptune Fountain, **5**, **6**, has
a similar purpose. It bridges the
corner between a high building
and a low one as well as acting as
a gateway to the greenery beyond.
From the top of the largest
building we see the main exit from
the square through a triumphal
arch, **8**, leading to another square.

8

1

2

3   **4**

The triumphal arch is flanked by
rows of shops, **1**; beyond we see a
tree-lined open space, **2**, **3**.
Smaller gateways on the other side
of the arch, **4**, continue the feeling
of enclosure, while more wrought
iron screens and low walls
surround the central area, **6**. Here
we find only simple dwelling
houses. At the end of this long
street-like space we approach an
oval piazza, **7**, formed by a
palatial building and its curved
colonnades, **10**. From the steps in
front of the building we look
back, **9**. Through the openings in
the colonnade we see the streets
and houses outside, **8**, **11**.

5

6

7

8   9

10 11

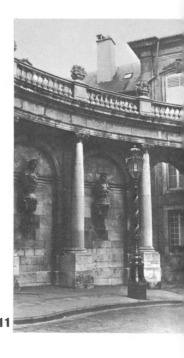

It is generally agreed that the Baroque did not
take root in the British Isles, and there are very
few true Baroque buildings in this country. This
is only to be expected, for the Baroque, as we have
seen, owed much of its impetus to the Catholic
Church and autocratic forms of government,
neither of which held sway in Britain. Yet in spite
of this the Baroque, because it was an expression of
the thoughts and feelings of the period and not
just a tool of these two powers, had a certain effect
on British architecture, art and town design. It
was, however, modified by more traditional
attitudes.

Christopher Wren was undoubtedly a Baroque
architect, although he worked in a Protestant and
non-authoritarian country. The façade of St. Paul's
displays many of the characteristics of Baroque
architecture, especially in the bizarre towers, **1**,
which have much in common with Borromini's
architecture. But only by looking at the plan of
this church, **4**, can we get an idea of the spatial
organisation. We then see that it resembles a
medieval church, **5**, rather than the great
continental Baroque models. This was not entirely
Wren's intention. As his earlier design for St. Paul's
shows, he intended to build a more Baroque church,
2, **3**, with a centralised ground plan and curved walls.
But this idea was rejected by the Anglican clergy.

1

2   **3**

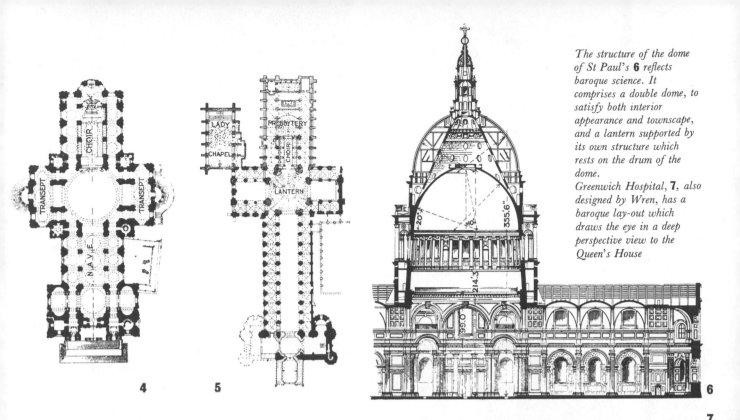

The structure of the dome of St Paul's **6** reflects baroque science. It comprises a double dome, to satisfy both interior appearance and townscape, and a lantern supported by its own structure which rests on the drum of the dome.

Greenwich Hospital, **7**, also designed by Wren, has a baroque lay-out which draws the eye in a deep perspective view to the Queen's House

4

5

6

7

2

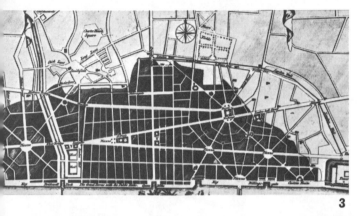

3

Wren's ideas on town design also show definite Baroque tendencies. After the Great Fire of London, which devastated a large area of the city, he produced a plan for re-building, **3**. He tried to eliminate the old, still largely medieval London, which had existed before the fire, **1**, **2**, and to apply the Baroque concepts of large, unified streets in a system designed for display and movement. The centrepiece of his design was the Stock Exchange. St. Paul's was set aside from the centre, as though to keep it away from the world of temporal power. Like the early design for St. Paul's, this plan was not approved, and instead the city was re-built on much more traditional lines. Picture **4** shows a typical street in re-built London, Fenchurch Street. It still had much in common with medieval streets: individual houses in an irregular pattern without the unifying overall pattern of Baroque planners. London remained largely a city of individual houses with a most unmistakable human scale.

1 *Medieval London at the time of Henry VIII. In the foreground is Ludgate Hill leading to the old St Paul's, finally destroyed in the fire of 1666.*

4

The British attitude to town design was confirmed by successive generations, especially by the people of the eighteenth century. The great Georgian developments in many British towns, such as London, Bath and Edinburgh, were essentially medieval and humane. They were based on a series of open spaces and squares, linked by short streets to form a pattern not so dissimilar from that of a medieval town, in which one could wander from space to space, and roam at will without being drawn to a visual focus or centrepiece. The aerial view of Bloomsbury, **1**, although photographed in the twentieth century, still shows the basic layout as it existed in the eighteenth century. It is one large, harmonious complex of wide and narrow spaces, buildings and trees, natural and man-made patterns.

An English square may have much in common with continental ones and was often influenced by them, but the basic idea was derived from different values. The open space was not regarded as a setting for a monument of the monarch in his rôle

1

2   3

as hero. The Place Royale in Paris, **2**, for example, had houses arranged round a royal monument in absolute uniformity like a platoon of soldiers, each one putting forward his best face. The English square, **3**, by contrast, was rather a civic space, designed for the convenience of all the inhabitants of the square, whose houses expressed a certain uniformity in the interests of the community but were not without individual variations. The place of the focal monument, the symbol of absolutism, was taken by trees and shrubs, irregularly arranged, a symbol of the Englishman's love of nature. It is significant that there was no need for a centre or focus.

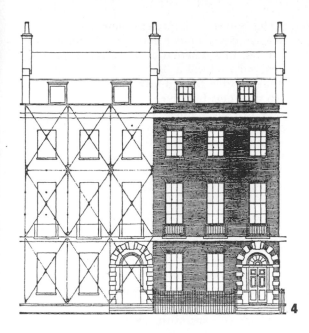

4

The interior of the houses could be varied to suit individual buyers, but had to conform to certain by-laws which enforced certain standards of structure, safety and hygiene. For instance, lightshafts, which were such an outstanding feature of continental housing, were not allowed in Britain.

The Georgian town house was above all a piece of functional design in which the needs of family life were related to what was normally a narrow site. Its proportions were the outcome of considerable thought, as the drawing, **4**, shows, but these visual considerations were at the service of functional requirements, **5**. This is why Georgian civic design was always based on the human scale, both in the exteriors of buildings and also in the design of staircases and furniture, **6**. Elegance and practical considerations here go hand in hand.

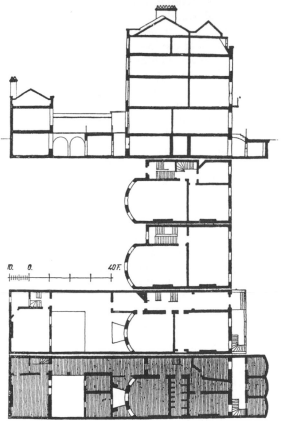

5   **6**

1

2

In the bigger and more impressive schemes of Georgian town development, Baroque elements may be noticed, but in a different context. We have seen that the curved wall was a Baroque device. This was, like many other foreign inventions, taken over by English designers but given a typically English emphasis. When the younger Wood in 1767 designed the Royal Crescent in Bath he took over this idea but put it to use to stress the relationship between building and site, for the curvature outlines the contours of the slope on which the Crescent stands. This results in a harmony between building and site not often found in speculative building. The giant pilasters are another Baroque feature. The straight connecting streets between the open spaces and the use of a round piazza, the Circus, as a meeting point of several streets is also Baroque, although on a human scale. The small, intimate doors and ground floor windows, the side streets with their shops, often allocated to pedestrian traffic only, are yet part of the overall plan. In the Georgian era town planning can be said to have reached a very high standard and many of the ideas incorporated in these designs are still followed in many of our present day developments. If we look in detail at a town such as Bath, which was largely built during the eighteenth century, we feel that all the past experience of town design seems to have been assimilated and compounded into one scheme. The overall harmonious pattern based on human measurements and needs is ever-present in Bath. We feel that the rambling, cellular medieval town has influenced this design. The Renaissance notion of unification and greater spatial consciousness is also here. The Baroque ideas of *dynamic* space, that is, space experienced by moving through it, and related through vistas from street to street, from space to space, are also incorporated here. All these have been related to each other, as an engineer would relate the various working parts of a machine to make it function efficiently. At the time when it was built, it represented the best that the human mind could devise as a setting for a civilised community.

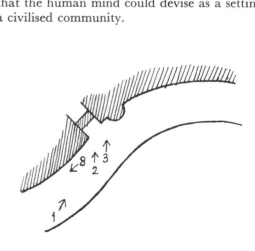

3

4

5

6

7

These pictures of Lansdown Crescent in
Bath show its baroque qualities. The
façade has a double curvature with a
small bulging curve accentuating the
point where it changes direction. As we
climb the hilly street, **1**, the Crescent
comes into view and reveals unsuspected
views in depth, **2**. Curves harmonise and
enhance each other, **3**. Looking back we
see the façade curve away in the opposite
direction to the Crescent proper, **8**, in a
gentle spiral. The town, the country, and
human needs are linked in one
comprehensive design.

Other parts of Bath show different
aspects of this attitude to the urban
environment. Imposing buildings, **4**, **5**, are
interspersed with more intimate
thoroughfares, **6**; nor have the backs of
houses been neglected, **7**.

8

1   **2**

3   **4**

5   **6**

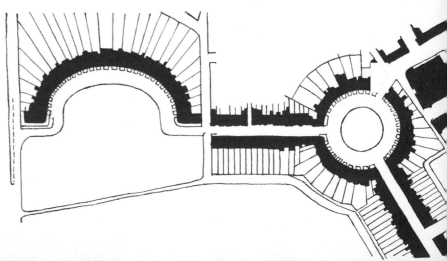

The plan shows the relationship between
the Royal Crescent and the Circus.
The Royal Crescent is approached
sideways, **1**, **2**; the full view is not
obtained until the corner has been
turned, **3**, **4**. The grandiose facade,
6, **7**, holds intimate human dwellings, **5**.
Another row of houses, **8**, links the
Royal Crescent to the landscape.

4 The industrial town and the Modern Movement

While the Georgian town schemes were being developed, a great change was taking place which was to deal a severe blow to the whole concept of the town, and all but extinguish it as a workable organism: this was the Industrial Revolution. Factories, a new element in the human environment, began to make their appearance all over the country. They were at first water-driven and often tucked away in the landscape, so that it was possible to see a certain romantic charm in these largely isolated additions to the human environment, **1**. But soon the Revolution gathered momentum, the invention of steam power opened up new possibilities of expansion, and whole industrial colonies sprang up near the coalfields, the sources of the new power. Favourably placed towns grew at an undreamt-of rate. Nothing was allowed to stand in the way of this expansion, everything was sacrificed to it. It was the age of the enterprising individual, the age of *laissez faire*, of unprecedented opportunity for some people and abject misery for many others. One cannot tell whether such rapid change would have occurred if initiative had been in the hands of the whole community, at any rate it was the individual and individual enterprise which dominated the development of our towns during the nineteenth century. The planning of the town had to give way to the needs of the moment. If industrial installation encroached on the landscape, so much the worse for the landscape; if it disfigured the face of the town, it was excused on grounds of expediency, if back-to-back housing created insanitary living conditions, well, human beings simply had to put up with them, they were considered an unavoidable by-product of progress. The enormous energy which went into every aspect of the Industrial Revolution, which made discoveries in technology and applied the new scientific ideas, had little thought or power to spare to add creatively to the towns, as past ages had done.

1

2

1 *Sheffield in 1801*
2 *The Black Country in 1866*
3 *Manchester in 1857*

3

1

2

3

Instead, railway lines were allowed to cross towns, often without viaducts; human habitations were surrounded by industrial plant, coke ovens, kilns, coal pits. Unhealthy conditions were created from which the majority were never able to break free. What is more, the result was a scene of visual chaos, and therefore ugliness, which is unparalleled in history.

Before the Industrial Revolution men's lives were ruled and adorned by certain natural rhythms. Houses were built in a way best suited to the nature of the land, normally of materials which reflected the natural resources of the environment. It was possible to see the landscape round the town from many vantage points, between houses, or above the roofline, and the landscape often invaded the confines of the town in the form of open spaces and patches of greenery. The rhythm of the seasons added a natural pattern to the lives of the townspeople. But now towns were created in which these patterns and rhythms were noticeably absent. With the rise of the railways brick became the cheapest building material, and this dealt a death blow to traditional building skills. Streets were made up according to the needs of industry or the convenience of developers. Landscape and seasons had little meaning when the air and ground were fouled and blighted by the excrements of industry: smoke, fumes, soot, dust, filth. The haphazard and irresponsible development of towns and the lack of regard they showed for basic human needs made them inefficient and almost unbearable places to live in.

1 *London*
2 *Manchester*
3 *Newcastle*
4 *Preston. Workers' cottages with an open sewer between them*
5 *Rochdale*
6 *Oldham. The last two pictures show that neglect of civic and residential areas has reached well into the twentieth century— a habit which dies hard*

4

5 6

The Industrial Revolution had produced the need for new types of buildings, factories, railway stations, warehouses, etc., all of which posed many new problems. What appearance should they have? Should they be made to look like other buildings? If so, what style, Romanesque, Gothic, Renaissance? There was no precedent for such buildings; solutions could not be found by consulting the architecture of the past. Cast iron and later steel made their appearance as building materials, and this added still further to the confusion. Architects had been trained in the principles of architecture derived from the Renaissance, but now they were confronted by the need for new types of buildings whose functions they did not quite understand. Even if they could understand them, they probably disliked them. They were confronted too with new building materials which could not be applied to the column, beam, arch, pediment, pilaster, the architectural elements with which they were acquainted. How can a factory be built of iron in an historic style?

1

2

3

The ensuing confusion, and the arguments which sought to settle it, sound ridiculous to us now. The Bible was invoked against iron as a building material; moral conceptions such as Sacrifice, Truth, Obedience were advanced as the guiding lights of architects. The industrialist could now show his piety by building his residence in the pious Gothic style. Towns which, as a result of industrial expansion had grown large enough to merit a charter, tried to emulate their medieval predecessors by building their new civic buildings in a style from the past, in order not to be outshone by the historic centres of older towns. This was also the result of the unpleasantness of contemporary industrial life, which made people recoil from anything even vaguely reminiscent of the present. Gradually visual sensibility was replaced by irrelevant moral issues and by sentimentality. Buildings were supposed to look noble or dignified, but the relationship of their parts was no longer considered with informed judgement as it had been in the past. For example, although Renaissance buildings were indeed designed to give an impression of nobility or piety, these qualities were expressed in terms of visual relationships and visual harmony. This confusion of visual values affected all man-made objects. The products of the machine were encrusted with meaningless ornaments which had nothing to do with the materials they were made of or the process by which they were manufactured. Painting and sculpture, as accepted by society, were likewise based on moral rather than visual values. During all the vital phases of European art, visual ideas and concepts had been enlarged: perspective and chiaroscuro helped Renaissance man to gain a clearer idea of the world; visual movement gave the Baroque a method of manipulating it. But now no new visual discoveries were made by the accepted artists, by those who shaped the environment. The intense feelings which in the past had made such discoveries inevitable were now absent. Their place was taken by mere sentimentality.

Townscape suffered immeasurably as a result of this confusion. Things were either left to take care of themselves or they were disguised in various historical costumes. ('Disguise is the spice of life' wrote a Victorian architect.) The question as to which of the various historical styles was best was never settled, but the 'Battle of the Styles' made the town into a vast battlefield, which can still be inspected in almost any part of Britain. Renaissance town halls and offices, Gothic schools and hospitals, often ill-lit and badly laid out, are still there for all to see. In the façades of buildings self-consciously revived, distorted styles vied with each other and left the townscape irreparably damaged. The Battle of the Styles raged just as fiercely inside the houses.

4   **5**   **6**

7   **8**

9

1 *A residential block*
2 *A street in London showing contrasting styles*
3 *A factory*
4 *A hospital*
5 *An office building*
6 *An office building*
7 *A row of dwellings*

Most man-made things were artificially styled, such as the 'Moorish' fork, **9**, *and the 'Gothic' door handle,* **8**.

Before we decide whether such attempts to revive the styles of the past are desirable or not, let us stop for a moment in our history of the town and consider the part which art plays in the man-made environment.

The origin of art is thought to have something to do with the recognition of known or imagined features in certain natural shapes, such as rocks or tree trunks. It is easy to recognise fantastic human and animal forms in such random objects, **1**. The next step might be to help this similarity on a little. A few deft strokes with the right tool, **2**, or a few daubs, would make the object even more recognisable, and so, step by step, a particularly creative person might arrive at the point where he could start from scratch and not wait for nature to provide him with a starting point. He had become an artist. His activity, which started with the attempt to make found or seen objects more recognisable, was an act of integration bringing thought and feeling together.

To a simple person an unknown or ambiguous object, especially one which reminds him of something actual or imagined, is often a source of fear. By bringing out this hidden image, by means of sculpture or painting, even if the image is a monster, he comes to terms with his own fears. It is better to know the worst; it is better to make the rock more like the fearsome spectre it seemed at first rather than suffer the torture of uncertainty. By making it recognisable, by making the unknown familiar, through sculpture or painting, the cause of the fear may be tamed. The act of creation is also an act of integration, an attempt to bring inner fear and outer reality into unison, to satisfy both reason and emotion at the same time and in one object. Here then we have the basic quality and the very function of all art: the integration of thought and feeling. It is an activity which is necessary to human beings in their day to day living; not a luxury but a vital balancing mechanism without which life would be—and often is—immeasurably harder or in some cases even impossible.

This basic principle—the desire for integration, bringing together of several aspects of man's mind and personality—can be seen in all the arts of the different periods in history. For instance, we have seen how early pottery vessels imitated the shapes of earlier ones, such as those made of leather (Part Two, page 68). This was due not only to an inability to produce a more efficient shape, but to a process similar to that which created the earliest sculpture: an attempt to give a strange, unknown

1

2

3

material a familiar look. When the character of the new material is understood, largely through repeated working, which makes it more familiar, these imitative shapes are abandoned. They no longer fit in with the state of mind of both maker and user, for familiarity and knowledge have replaced uncertainty and fear. The true character of the material can now be allowed to manifest itself. Pottery can now develop its own shapes; the old shapes no longer act as a bridge between mind and material, for the mental attitudes have changed.

This, basically speaking, is the reason why art changes throughout the ages: it must change when materials or mental attitudes change, if it is to remain efficient as a bridge between reason and the emotions. The Baroque was just as efficient in its own period as was the Gothic before it. But both were efficient only while the conditions which made them necessary existed.

When, during the Industrial Revolution, the Gothic and Renaissance visual languages were revived the conditions which had brought them into being had long since disappeared. How could a Gothic railway station 'speak' to a traveller or a railway worker in the way the Gothic buildings of the Middle Ages had spoken to their communities? The Gothic method of building had been evolved in order to solve certain problems, but what problems could a Gothic railway station solve? How could it make the structure accessible to the emotions as its historic prototypes had done? Very few people who used these buildings could be fully involved with them because of the appearance which their builders chose for them. The appearance of these man-made things did not bridge thought and feeling. On the contrary, the imposition of an arbitrary form, unsuited to the times, did more damage than if the builders had allowed the function of a building to decide its appearance. In their confusion, lacking as they did a visual language of their own, the architects of the nineteenth century chose the appearance of their buildings by an act of the will. The visual languages of the great periods of art of the past had never been imposed by an act of the will; they sprang from inner needs, from feeling rather than from thought, although reason took a prominent part in their development.

4   5

1 *An old tree trunk, perhaps suggestive of an animal head*
2 *Early 'sculpture'. A human shape suggested by the formation of the stone. The hidden image is made recognisable*
3 *Ritual objects with magic decorations*
4 *Spearhead with rivets. The tang is retained from an earlier form, the rivets in turn will be retained even when they are no longer necessary—they have an emotional as well as a mechanical purpose. (See The Development of Shape, page 12)*
5 *The modern cruet ties thought and feeling like the earlier examples: mathematical precision and sensuous realisation of form*

While architects, always looking to the past, failed to develop a visual language, the engineers of the nineteenth century carried on the traditional rôle of the artist. The great engineers made proper use in their buildings and bridges of the materials which technology gave them. They employed them in a wholly original way, understanding their character and marrying them to the function of the structure. The new shapes of railway stations, **1**, exhibition halls, **2**, bridges, and other structures were not dictated by any feelings of nobility or piety, as were many of the contemporary examples of 'real' architecture, but by the nature of the materials, the function of the structure, and the needs of the people who were to use them. As the artists of the past had done, these engineers developed new visual concepts which summed up and expressed ideas already in the air.

Cast iron and later steel lent themselves to tenuous structures, made possible because the forms of the structures were entirely suited to the materials which composed them. The *form* thus became a visual manifestation of the structure and not something arbitrarily and wilfully imposed upon it. The roof of a railway station, for instance, could now be made of a web-like system of metal girders and supports. Because it weighed only a fraction of what a stone-vaulted roof would weigh, it could span a greater area. The form of the roof was dictated by the demands of both material and function.

Although engineering structures were often hidden or given an 'architectural' front of more traditional appearance, they were an honest expression of the new elements of the human environment. Architects, by contrast, used the visual languages of past ages. Such elements as columns, buttresses, and even pinnacles simply had to be introduced because they were the 'words' of the traditional visual language. Even though they were no longer necessary, architects had to pretend that they were, and this often led to ludicrous situations.

The techniques engineers employed were wholly in keeping with their understanding of the new materials and the visual thinking derived from them. When Benjamin Baker, one of the designers of the Firth of Forth Bridge, heard that the bridge had been criticised because the two central arches did not continue in a smooth curve, as the arches of other bridges, he replied that the 'arches' were cantilevers; to have made them like arches when in fact they rested on different principles altogether would have been to deny them their proper character. We might add that it would have been a visual lie. But the new structures did not merely express new ideas about new techniques and new materials. An age which had been staggered by the theory of evolution must also have sensed certain similarities between nature's methods and the attempts of engineers to build efficiently: the likeness between natural organisms and a structure such as the telescope gallery of the Crystal Palace, **2**.

1

2

It was the work of engineers, therefore, that expressed in a most vital manner the thoughts and feelings of their times. When architects began to use iron and steel in their designs they had the experience of the engineers to draw upon. Soon the new materials were accepted in their own right. The American architect Louis Sullivan used cast iron in the Carson Pirie Scott store in Chicago, **3**, to obtain advantages, such as lightness of structure and large windows, which he could not have obtained by any other means. In spite of the profusion of ornaments, the structural members are dominant in this building. Architecture had become art again, and was no longer a masquerade.

3

1

2

These developments, leading to the introduction
of new materials and new thoughts about the
man-made environment, took place at the same
time as another, parallel movement whose aim
was to rescue the best of the past. When William
Morris had his Red House built, **1**, and set up in
business as a firm of craftsmen, he was attempting
to counter not only the inhumanity of the
industrial town, but also the ugliness of machine-
made goods, and of houses built for cheapness
without the traditional knowledge which in the
past had made even humble dwellings visually
significant and pleasing. He did not at first believe
that the machine could improve the quality of life,
and although he later revised his ideas he never
fully accepted the machine as such. But the example
he set of starting from first principles and
producing goods of sound craftsmanship with an
understanding of basic functions, working, in other
words, as the craftsmen of the past had done, was
not without effect. Charles Voysey produced
houses, furniture and even wallpaper of a type
which combined the simplicity of the best of the
past with the modern spirit of functionalism (an
attitude which demands that the appearance of
things should express their function). Gimson
designed chairs, **2**, which were as good as anything
produced in the past and probably stand up to the
best produced by the most eminent designers of the
twentieth century.

The most outstanding figure to emerge from this
period, which can now be seen to occupy a
position between old and modern, on either side of
the threshold of the twentieth century, was the
Scotsman Charles Rennie Mackintosh.

The Glasgow School of Art, designed in 1897,
is his chief work. If we compare its front elevation,
3, with that of the Red House we see at once that
here a new language is spoken, a new era
anticipated, perhaps even ushered in. Its structure
and purpose are plain to see; they are stated with a
frankness which must have shocked those who
believed that in architecture, as in life, the facts of
life should be hidden. It has a stark, functional
appearance, whilst the structure is expressed,
especially inside the building, by clearly defined
timber beams and posts, masonry arches and piers,
4. If anything, the structure is over-stated and made
more explicit than necessary. We must remember,
however, that the building was designed at a time
when 'good taste' demanded that the bones of a
building should be hidden; it was a revolt against
this convention. The building is devoid of the
usual architectural elements, such as pilasters and
pediments. The wrought iron brackets on the
façade are intended to act as supports for the
window cleaner's ladder. But Mackintosh contrived
to wring a decorative and spatial meaning from

3

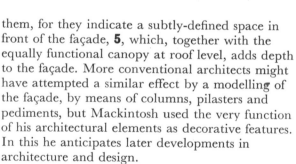

5

them, for they indicate a subtly-defined space in front of the façade, **5**, which, together with the equally functional canopy at roof level, adds depth to the façade. More conventional architects might have attempted a similar effect by a modelling of the façade, by means of columns, pilasters and pediments, but Mackintosh used the very function of his architectural elements as decorative features. In this he anticipates later developments in architecture and design.

The library of the School of Art, **6**, added in 1907, is in many ways the most significant part of the building. The supports of the upper gallery are not placed immediately beneath it but join the beams well outside it. Again the structure is shown: paired beams on short posts joined to the taller posts which support the roof. The gallery is structurally joined to the rest of the building, it is an integrated design. But the method also has other purposes, visual rather than structural. Had the posts been immediately beneath the gallery, they would have created a narrow, mean space round the library, but by taking the beam out into the central space a more generous subsidiary space is created, more than a corridor, and one which harmonises better with the overall space of the library. This new feeling for space, which can be sensed in all Mackintosh's work, make him a true pioneer of the Modern Movement.

6

1

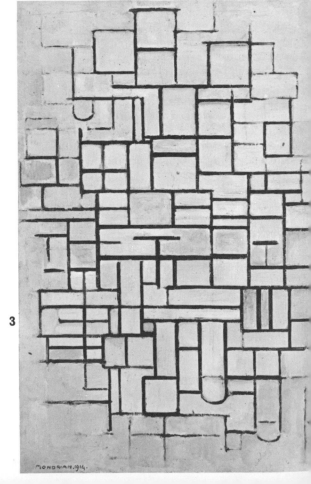

2   3

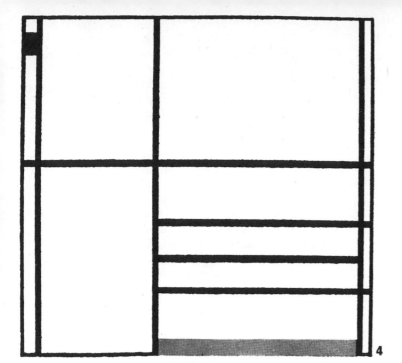

4

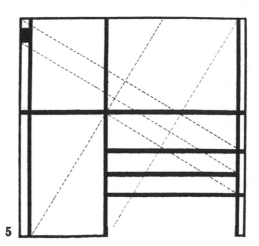

5

We have already discussed, in Part Three, how modern analytical attitudes led to Cubism, but there were still other forms of visual analysis. In picture **1** you see a painting by the Dutch artist, Mondriaan. It is a still life and consists of a group of objects on a table. Some of the objects are recognisable: a covered jar, a couple of books, tumblers, a pan, a white cloth; others are not so recognisable but they have been incorporated in a general visual impression of the scene. In the second painting, of a similar subject, **2**, the moulding of recognisable objects into one overall impression has been taken a step further. It looks as though the artist had attempted to bring order to his impression of the scene, for the painting is now much more sorted out. Mondriaan has broken down the individual shapes and reconstituted them in an ordered pattern; he has also related the shapes to the shape of the painting itself; many of the lines are parallel to the sides of the frame, and are either vertical or horizontal. Several shapes or lines are repeated or reflected in other parts of the painting, creating a rhythm which moves within the stricter patterns of uprights and horizontals. This painting is a form of visual analysis of what the artist has seen, an investigation, by visual means, into the nature of his visual experience, and the derivation of a logical image from this experience. The purely visual relationships have been clarified—the vision explained. In the third painting reality as such has been abandoned and what remains is the pattern made up of visual elements whose relationships the artist has analysed, **3**. In spite of the severity of the geometry the effect is rather playful.

Picture **4** shows an even later painting by Mondriaan in which visual relationships have been further refined through complete abstraction and geometric balance. The large rectangle in the left-hand bottom corner is in the golden proportion and the rest of the composition is derived from it. This new kind of visual analysis was not confined to painting. The architect Theo van Doesburg made many researches into the nature of form and space, such as, **6**, which was considered by him not so much as an exercise in construction *techniques* as in construction *thoughts*.

6

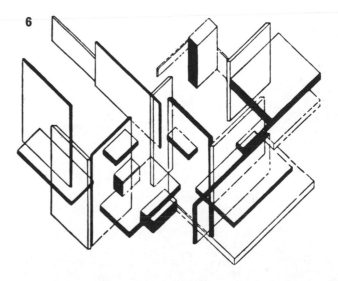

Rietveld, the Dutch architect, had obviously also thought about a house in an analytical way, taking it to pieces in order to understand it, and then assembling it in such a way that his visual analysis was quite obvious to anyone who looked at it, **1**. Artists of this period thought it most important that other people should understand their new ideas, so that a building like this one was not only a house but also a statement about a house. The relationships of the different parts had to be shown clearly, very much as in the work of Mondriaan and Mackintosh, so that people might understand them. Rietveld also designed a chair, **2**. Again we must not judge it purely as a chair, but as a modern *idea* of a chair, an analysis of a chair and of the structural purpose of the members. The similarity between this and the structure of the gallery of Mackintosh's School of Art are obvious.

The pictures you see on these two pages are examples of *visual thinking*, outstanding not only as works of art in their own right, but also because they taught people, including other artists, a great deal about the modern attitude to structure, and the methods of modern visual analysis. It is obvious that these ideas had an important bearing on other developments. The designs of engineers which were based on a technological analysis of structure were confirmed by a visual analysis of structure. From Morris onwards forms were stripped of all unnecessary ornament, but this in itself would have come to nothing if the basic forms had not been analysed and as a result reconstituted. None of the modern ideas we have discussed so far could by themselves have produced a modern architecture. They had to join and fall into a pattern in which each played a relevant part.

2

*Rietveld's house is not merely a façade. The same structural thought and visual analysis are evident inside, **3**. Forms and space are organised.*

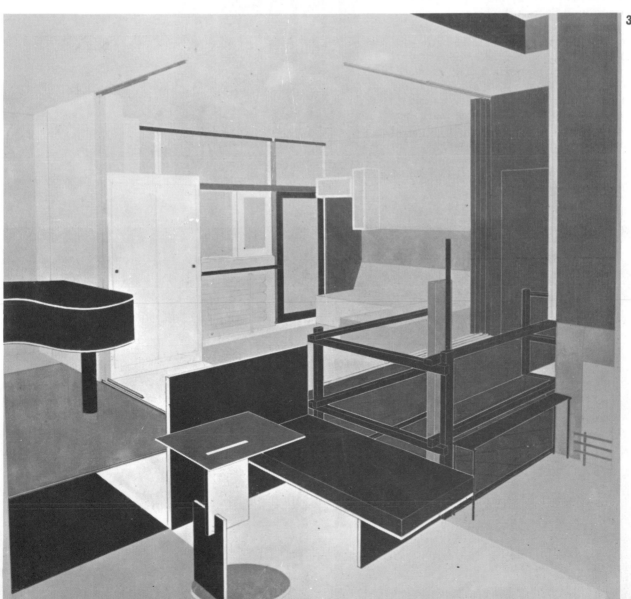

3

When reinforced concrete was introduced as a
building material its character was soon given
visual expression. One of the earliest pioneers
of reinforced concrete, the Frenchman Auguste
Perret, not only thoroughly understood this
character, but he also had the benefit of a
limited but workable visual language, so that in
his works the new material, its character and
associated techniques begin to find suitable
expression. The house shown in picture **1**
was designed by him in 1904. It shows a realisation
of the advantages and character of reinforced
concrete, expressed in an appropriate visual
language. The framework of the building is never
hidden, on the top floor it comes out into the open,
so that the balconies can be seen as natural parts
of the overall structure and not mere additions.
All the parts of the building are visually related to
each other. The hollowed-out façade, with its
cantilevers over the entrances, gives a sense of
lightness which is stressed by the large expanse of
glass on the ground floor, just where one would
normally have expected the greatest structural
strength and the thickest members. The ground
floor plan of this house shows the obvious
advantages of the new material, **2**. The structure
consists of posts and beams; walls are for infill only
and this fact is expressed on the façade by the
decorative patterns of the walls, which mark them
as non-load-bearing. Inside, the new structural
ideas mean that walls can be placed almost-
anywhere, preferably between any two pillars, to
suit the convenience of the occupants. The staircase
has a wall of glass bricks.

1

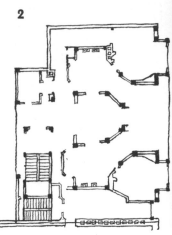

2

3

4

It was not until the Centennial Hall in Breslau, Germany, **3, 4**, was designed by Max Berg in 1913 that reinforced concrete came fully into its own as a building material which gave the architect the opportunity to be both artist and engineer. He was now able not only to produce a structure for the uses of modern society, by using the resources of modern technology, but also to express his thoughts and feelings about material and structure. The Centennial Hall is the first important essay in the real potentialities of reinforced concrete. Its forms are wholly original and are calculated to make the best use of the material in a visually exciting form. While modern architecture was evolving towards a more articulate visual language, based on the methods and needs, the thoughts and feelings of the time, town design based on modern architectural principles also took an important step forward.

The insanitary conditions and the general difficulties associated with life in industrial towns caused many outcries—and also a number of plans of how town life, which had apparently got out of hand, might be reorganised in new and humane conditions. Chief amongst the urban reformers of the nineteenth century was Ebenezer Howard, who in his book 'Tomorrow' (1898) set out his ideas of the structure of a modern new town. His plan was based on the Renaissance ideal of centralisation, **5**. A central garden of five acres was to be surrounded by civic and administrative buildings; by another park, in the form of a ring; by a glass arcade, called the Crystal Palace, for the display of manufactured goods; a grand avenue 400 feet wide; an agricultural belt; allotments, and the railway line. Houses standing in their own gardens were to be interspersed between these concentric rings. Several such cities were then to be linked up in a larger system, **6**.

The plan was essentially backward-looking. In seeking a solution to the problems of contemporary life, caused by the machine and the factory system, reformers such as Howard and William Morris held up the medieval town as the only possible pattern for communal life. But this did not help to solve anything in the long run. The Garden City Movement which sprang from Howard's plans envisaged not only a near-medieval organisation but even a medieval appearance of the new town, **7**. Industry and all the other manifestations of the machine age were grudgingly accommodated in the new planning, instead of being made a vital element in it.

5

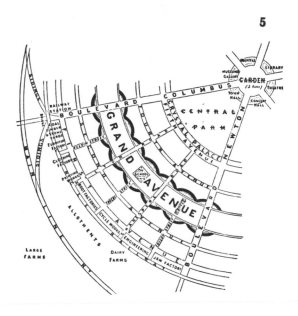

6

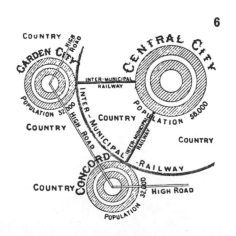

7

In 1901 the French architect Tony Garnier drew up plans for a modern industrial town of 35,000 inhabitants, **5**. A first glance at this will show that here we have the first really modern town design, one which appreciates the problems of a modern town and grapples with them in a modern way. By comparison, Ebenezer Howard's design must appear amateurish, for all its good intentions. Unlike Howard's design, it is not a diagram, based on historical precedent, but a plan whose very essence is based on topographical features, social and individual requirements, making realistic provision for industry and transport, and solidifying these ideas into concrete form, reinforced concrete to be precise.

As the plan shows, the different functions and services, industry, housing, entertainment, sport, transport, health services, etc., are differentiated. The industrial area is completely separated from the residential one. Hospitals are also set apart in the most favourable position, on a slope facing south. There is a speedway and a sports arena. Trains enter the station underground. There are many other advanced ideas in this design.

Tony Garnier did not leave this as a theoretical plan, he gave it full architectural expression, dealing with a modern problem in a modern way, abandoning all those ideas of the past which had no relevance to the twentieth century. He proposed to give it a modern shape by modern methods, using reinforced concrete. A building such as the station, **2**, for example, would have been impossible in any other medium. This project is a true visual expression of the way in which the problem of the modern industrial town has been considered and solved.

Even by today's standards these structures are wholly satisfactory, and at the time when they were designed they were advanced and prophetic. Note how the sculpturesque construction of integrated roof and pillar is left bare, **1**; note also the openings to admit light. The reinforced concrete shapes of our own day have here been anticipated. We must remember that in 1901 Garnier had no precedents to guide him and had to rely on imagination and intellect. Not all his buildings have this very advanced character, some lean on traditional shapes, **4**, but even here the open staircases and roof gardens and asymmetrical layout are wholly modern. We might today criticise the layout of the residential blocks as too severely geometric, but they are designed to avoid the main thoroughfares so that the whole town could be crossed without touching the residential streets.

3

4

5
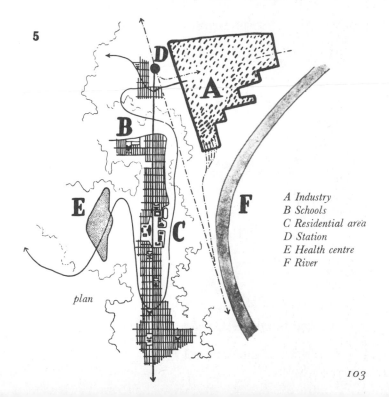

A *Industry*
B *Schools*
C *Residential area*
D *Station*
E *Health centre*
F *River*

plan

1 *The town hall*
2 *The station*
3 *The courtyard of house*
4 *A residential street*

This plan for a modern industrial town was never carried out, but it contained the seeds of many things to come. It exerted a powerful influence on town designers almost up to the present day. (Tony Garnier did, however, carry out a number of smaller designs of the industrial town of Lyons.) The important aspect of the plan is that it combines planning for modern conditions with modern building techniques and modern visual ideas. Architecture was, at least here, no longer an isolated discipline, but an art wholly in the service of building a better *total* environment. Like his great predecessors of the past, Tony Garnier must have seen a town as a single design problem—a very large one but one in which nothing could be isolated—perhaps he even saw it as a work of art. He meant to leave as little as possible to chance. In his town all the buildings were to be related to each other in a harmonious, functional pattern and it was to be in the shapes dictated by modern building methods and materials and modern ideas about form.

Modern ideas about town design were thus expressed in their most important outlines at the beginning of this century. But for a complete realisation of twentieth-century thought yet another idea had to be thoroughly understood and related to others: movement.

We have already seen (Part Three, pages 103-106) how movement and its analysis acquired importance during the later nineteenth century and how it permeated the technology of those days. Before it could be properly understood in a visual sense and related to other elements of our environment it had to await artistic analysis. Paul Klee, to whom most modern visual ideas can be traced, analysed the nature of movement, and the ways in which it can be given visual expression. Movement could now be thought of as part of the character of an object. Duchamp's painting of a coffee grinder describes the object not only in terms of its shape, but also in terms of its movement, **1**. Its movement is a part of its character and of its presence. When Gropius designed a building he did not merely design a modern shape, but added movement, shown by the arrows, as a new dimension of form, **2**. Buildings were now designed which took account not only of people's needs but also of their movements. These new ideas had a profound influence on town planning.

When in 1913 the Italian architect Sant' Elia produced drawings which explained his ideas about the construction and organisation of new towns, movement was an essential ingredient in his designs, **3**, **4**. His buildings are linked by lines of communication, often at different levels. They are held together not only by spatial relationships but also by those of movements. This highly complex arrangement appears more like a machine than a town in the old sense. Sant' Elia aims, as did Garnier, at a total attitude to environment. His plans are not built-up bits and pieces. They constitute a highly prophetic message.

1

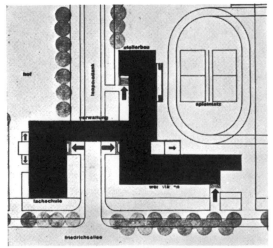

2

3

4

105

It was Le Corbusier who produced the first truly modern town designs. He said 'A house is a machine for living in' and his basic conception of a modern house, as shown in his drawing, **1**, is indeed that of a dwelling machine, in which nothing is introduced without a purpose. The house is designed with what were then (1924) advanced building methods in mind. The central supporting pillar rises like a tree trunk; floors, like branches, are cantilevered out from it. Since the floors take their support from the pillar, outer walls are now only for infilling, that is for keeping the weather out, and not for support. They can therefore be of plastic or some other non-structural material suitably insulated. There is no need for them to reach the floor, so that the ground can be left clear and one's view unimpeded. Children can play in the open spaces instead of using the streets; circulation in general is both easy and pleasant. The top floor can be used for all the services normally required as well as for a roof garden. This basic idea is directly derived from the new building techniques; it would have been impossible without them.

2 *Modern architecture need not distrupt the flowing lines of the landscape.*
3, **4** *Corbusier's early thoughts on traffic segregation*
5 *Corbusier's comparison of an old town with a well-planned modern town*

By adding together many such buildings, or others based on similar principles, so that they form a more complex machine, the town, Corbusier produces again 'a machine for living in', but on a wider level, for the whole community, with a more complex organisation, **6**. Such large buildings must have good communications, not only internally but also with each other. The whole town must have efficient lines of communication with other towns. Transport is required for people going to work, or to places of entertainment, for goods, mail, raw materials for industry and the finished products of the same industry, which employs all the people living in the town. Structure and movement are the basic ingredients in Le Corbusier's plan. Such an organisation for a large inhabited area can also allow for plenty of living space to move about in, open-air cafés, parks, etc., **5**. The town is now seen as a living organism on a gigantic scale, a twentieth century mechanism, designed for living and moving about in.

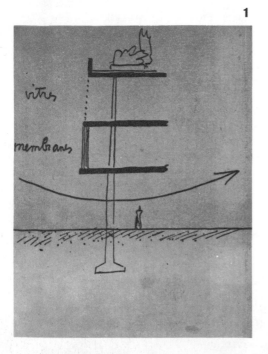

1

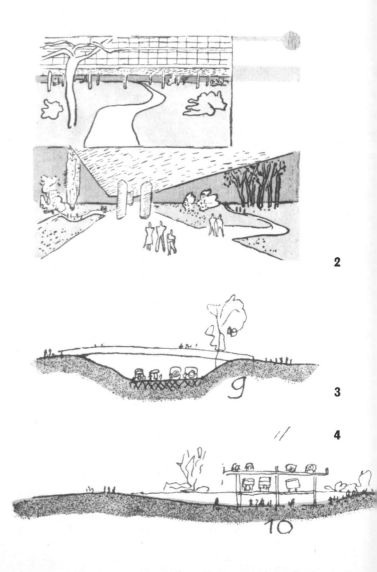

2

3

4

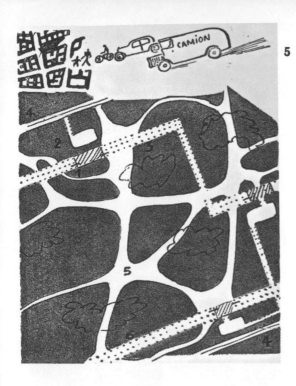

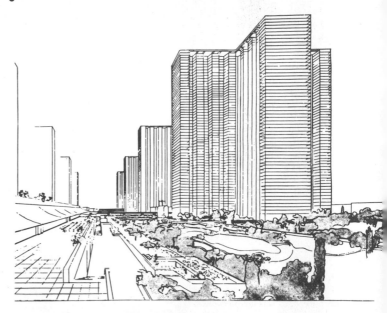

To follow the ideas of town design to the present day we must take another look at the development of modern architecture, for it is here that the elements of the modern town are evolved.

We have seen that modern architecture has some of its origins in the Industrial Revolution, which shaped the world and the society we live in. It owes much to the attempts of artists to replace the meaningless machine-made products of their time by intelligently and sensitively produced objects; to new materials and the efforts of engineers to make the best use of them by devising relevant shapes; to artists' visual analysis of form, space and movement. These are some of the most important influences; others are less tangible, inexpressible in words, but which can be felt when architecture is fully experienced.

Alvar Aalto's sanatorium in Finland, **7**, was designed in 1929. It is a bold reinforced concrete building whose structure is its only decorative feature. The material is handled with great assurance, much greater than, for instance, that of Perret (page 100). The different parts of the sanatorium, bedrooms, balconies, lift-shaft, etc., are given varied architectural expression, but the parts are held together as an organic whole. Inherent in this design is a great concern for the well being of the patients. The balconies are for communal use by small groups of patients, and not individually attached to single bedrooms; this expresses a new attitude to the psychology of sick people. Inside, the fittings are designed for efficiency and convenience, down to the last light switch, and are related to the whole. The whole complex building is informally sited among the pine trees.

1

2

3

The office building which Frank Lloyd Wright designed for the Johnson Wax Company in Racine, USA, in 1937, employs new forms which make no concessions to the traditional idea of what an office block should look like, **2**. Its bare walls have as their sole decoration the pattern of brickwork and the strips of glass tubes which admit the light instead of the usual windows. The form of support used for the bridge and several cantilevered parts, a column tapered towards the ground, is also seen inside the building, **1**. In the great central hall each column supports a circular section of the roof while the remaining roof area is filled in with tubular, heat-resistant glass. The lighting effect achieved by the combination of glass cornice and glass roof, together with the spatial effect of the tall columns only nine inches wide at the base, has been described as pure poetry in architecture. The building was a grand statement of modern architecture, and at the time it was built its effect must have been overwhelming. Looking at it now, nearly thirty years later, although we can still recognise it as great architecture, we might feel inclined to think some of the forms too arbitrary, too wilful, not yet precise and crisp enough for an architecture of the machine age. We can judge with hindsight, in the light of later developments in architecture, some of which we

shall discuss later. The fact remains that this building was absolutely right for its time, for it speaks the language of the 1930's. It was a most influential building and its effects are still felt today.

Corbusier's Law Courts building in Chandigarh, India, **3**, is of our own day. A whole generation lies between this and Frank Lloyd Wright's building, and the differences in architectural thought are evident. Its overall structure is precise and simple, but within this form we encounter the most astonishing complexities. The roof structure is supported by slabs; the space between them is completely filled by a pattern of reinforced concrete slabs designed to break the strong sunlight. Inside, a ramp leads to the upper floors. On the face of it the whole structure looks clear and calculated; everything could be justified in terms of function. The openings in the wall of the ramp look rather like the holes in the members of the frame of an aircraft, cut out to save unnecessary weight. But the more we look at it the more undercurrents of a biological nature seem to emerge. The façade —if this expression still applies—is really not so much reminiscent of engineering as of a microscopic view of a section of a natural organism made up of cells, such as skin. Even the vaulted roof makes biological allusions. And are the holes

in the wall merely to save weight or material, or to
let in the light? Or are they perhaps attempts to
open up wider perspectives, spatial relationships, **1, 2**
as in some of Henry Moore's sculpture **3**? Those
openings in sculptural forms have a decorative
value but they also serve to let us see through to
the other side, to get a sensuous understanding of
the form and to help us in our visual analysis of it.
When Corbusier adds an arrow to his building,
(**1**, page 106) he implies that we may look and
move through the opening he has left, in much the
same way as Moore implies that we should look
through to the other side of his sculpture.
Like all great works of art this building unites a
number of different thoughts and feelings. Our
understanding of the deeper workings of nature,
especially that part of nature which cannot be seen
with the naked eye, have given us an insight into
rhythms more profound than those which were
known or sensed in earlier times. We have also
gained a greater understanding of the human mind,
of the complex machinery which operates at very
deep levels of consciousness, and we realise the
falseness of so many conventions inherited from
the past. We are also beginning to understand the
connection between the biological and psychological
processes. We probe beneath the surface in a
scientific and also in an emotional sense, but we
are still far from certain what our findings so far
mean, nor can we guess what is still to be
discovered, digested and felt. Our lives are
dominated by three contrasting elements: by the
refined precision of mathematics and science, by
our growing awareness of the power of our
irrational selves and by the uncertainty and
emotional incompleteness of our quest. Many of
the works of art produced today echo these
conflicting feelings and ideas and try to reconcile
them as art has always done, by producing objects
which will satisfy them at the same time. Corbusier's
building, both in its overall design and in its
details has this purpose and effect. It has a stark
grandeur which hints at the dawn of human
history, the most primitive and powerful emotions,
and the unfathomable biological functioning of
natural organisms and their mystery and magic.
At the same time it has a precision expected by
people who have grown up in an industrial and
scientific society, a feeling for the character of
materials and their appropriate use, and the strength
to state these things honestly in rather the same
way as we are now able to say things in public
which would have made our parents wince. In this
building the traditional division between inside and
outside has been almost eliminated; space is infinite.
Solids and spaces are completely interlocked,
flowing into each other in many different forms.
The façade is tenuously defined, indicated only

by the edges of the sun break—the rest is space.
Let no one imagine that Corbusier designed this
building with all these motives in his conscious
mind. Art is never produced like that. It is true that
the intellect must play a vital part in the calculation
and construction of a building like this one, but the
driving force which makes the creation of a work
of art necessary and then suffuses it, stems from
feeling rather than thought. Corbusier felt, as many
of us do, all the things which we recognise in his
building, but because he felt them more deeply
and had the visual endowment and technical skill
to express them, he was able to produce a work of

art, a symbol of what we too feel but in an inarticulate way. We can identify ourselves with it at several levels. Technology and emotions justify each other.

We may look upon the Law Courts building in Chandigarh as one of the highest achievements of modern architecture. Successive architects will learn from it for many years but it has set almost impossibly high standards which it will be difficult to emulate. Yet the example is there.

When the architects James Stirling and James Gowan were asked to design the new engineering building for Leicester University they had many limiting factors to contend with. The site, an awkwardly shaped piece of ground left over after earlier building developments, was to accommodate workshops, laboratories, administrative offices, lecture theatres, and their facilities and services. Very important amongst the latter was the installation of a water tank which had to be placed at least a hundred feet above the ground to provide sufficient pressure for the experiments in the hydraulics laboratory. The layout of the workshops had to be kept flexible so that the interior arrangement could be altered without any structural changes. The workshops also required north lights because of the delicate nature of much of the equipment which, if exposed to direct sunlight, might be made less efficient or even permanently damaged. Because scientific equipment used in research quickly becomes obsolete and must be frequently replaced, provision for such replacement, often in the form of heavy machinery, had to be made in the design of the building. There were many other points to be considered: the inclusion of a second staircase to the larger of the lecture theatres, for instance, so that latecomers could reach the back of the theatre direct, and an exceptionally steep rake to the theatre so that all students could get a good top view of the experiments.

It must have seemed almost impossible to satisfy all the requirements of the university in one cluster of buildings which would at the same time look right for its purpose. But, as in many brilliantly solved design problems, it is those very difficulties which account for the best features of the solution: the finished building. The very fact that the shape of the plot would not permit of a building with one clear side facing north made it necessary to provide the required north lights in an original way. The roof lights do indeed face north, but their ridges run at an angle of $45°$ to the other sides. This produces a pattern of three-dimensional, intersecting shapes which is surprising, thrilling, and, especially at night, magical. The glass-sheathed spiral staircase in this picture is the second entry to the large lecture theatre. Because the building was not allowed to approach too close to the road, the laboratory block had to have its corner chamfered, producing a shape which, together with the north lights, forms a series of faces which balance the ridges of the workshop roof running at right angles to it. The functional requirements have been met in a most authoritative and visually significant manner. The water tank is housed in the top of the administrative building and their combined weight

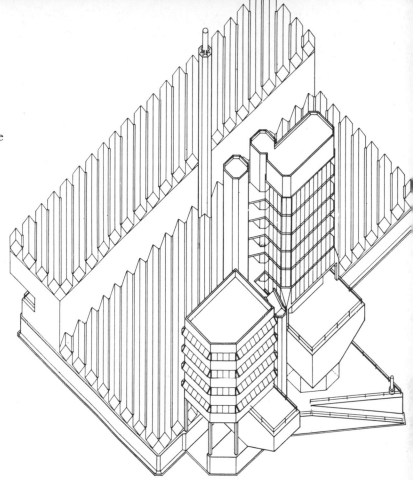

makes the cantilever of the large theatre possible. The laboratory block overhangs the service road, so that machinery can be hoisted straight from lorries by means of a gantry. The windows of the laboratory block are specially designed so that in the event of an experiment misfiring quick ventilation can be obtained by opening the lower, horizontal part of the window.

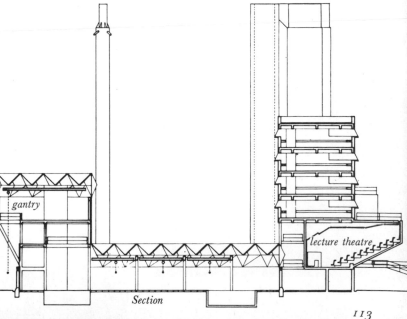

gantry

lecture theatre

Section

Details, such as the seats in the theatre, **2**, and the service pipes, **1**, have been designed with great care and play their part in the appearance of the building. At the other extreme, the disposition of the main masses of the building in three-dimensional space shows the touch of the master. All the shapes are arranged in a harmonious spatial relationship, based, no doubt, on the researches of the early pioneers such as Doesburg. The interplay of solids and voids, including the volumes contained by the transparent glass walls, is also significant. Note, page 112, the thrilling penetration of the large cantilevered theatre by the transparent spiral staircase. This was a functional requirement, but how exciting this union of two dissimilar shapes is! Such daring ideas ensure the organic unity of shapes designed for different functions.

We have noted before that modern buildings often emphasise the aspect of lightness. Perret's building, **1**, page 100, for instance, appears to be lighter at the bottom than at the top. The Leicester engineering building shares this quality. Its apparent base is a small area somewhere round the intersection of the sloping lines of the two theatres, and the resulting feeling of lightness is accentuated by the ethereal quality produced by so much glass. The space inside the building is enclosed by glass walls, **4**, often of a complex three-dimensional pattern, but the transparent walls do not contain it. This is a wholly modern conception of space.

3 *Lecture theatre.*
4 *Students leaving the building, seen through one of the many glass walls. The raked floor of the lecture theatre can be seen on the left and the trees in the park beyond. On the right the glass roof of the workshops is visible.*
5, **6** *Two views of the glass roof.*

1

2   3

4

5   6

The Nottingham Playhouse occupies a sloping site, and this has been turned to good advantage by the architect Peter Moro. The most obvious advantage is that the stalls can follow the slope of the ground. Furthermore, by placing the entrance at mezzanine level, between stalls and balcony, the burden of stair-climbing has been divided between those who have seats in the stalls and those using the balcony. Yet another advantage of the sloping ground is the overhang at the back of the theatre which forms a loading bay for the work-shops. The architects have therefore derived the maximum help in the planning of the theatre from a natural feature of the site which could easily, in less skilled hands, have become an embarrassment and a drawback. The functional aspect of the building is not hidden: the round drum of the auditorium is visible from the outside, rising up from its enclosing block comprising corridors, staircases, foyers and bars. The wall of the ground floor is transparent so that the inner structure can be seen.

The auditorium itself is circular. It is lined with wooden panels which can be adjusted to correct the acoustics; lights are placed behind it. Stage lighting is supplied from the edge of the balcony and from a suspended drum. The front of the stage is movable so that it can be adapted for use at three levels: as an extension of the stage, to provide additional stalls when moved level with the floor, and as an orchestra pit when lowered.

So much for the purely functional aspects, but the architects have produced more than just a theatrical machine. For instance the circular auditorium allows each person to see not only the stage but also a sizable section of the audience and this makes the feeling of belonging to a theatre audience witnessing a stage production much more powerful.

When the traditional picture frame stage is used—without the forestage—the stage is frameless, seen through a gap in the drum. It completes the drum so that actors and audience feel close together. In the more old-fashioned theatres excessive decoration, a framed stage and a wedge-shaped auditorium separate actors from audience.

The circulation areas—foyers and staircases—explore the spaces which surround the auditorium. The only real decoration is an aluminium cast mural which makes a three-dimensional pattern. This is especially useful because it is on the curved outer wall of the auditorium. Since from some angles the mural curves away and cannot be seen in its entirety, the three-dimensional character of the mural shows the continuity of the design round the curvature. There is no interior decoration as such and the building materials are exposed in most cases: concrete, glass, brick, metal. From the outside, and especially when the building is lit up, the upper storey appears to be floating like a halo round the drum-like heart of the theatre.

We have analysed a number of modern buildings. They may be wonderful in themselves but in the long run we must consider them as the elements of our environment, the bits and pieces from which towns are made. The visual significance of buildings may be destroyed by indifferent surroundings, and even a number of good buildings may be combined unsuccessfully, so that instead of enhancing each other they detract from each other and minimise each other's stature. We must now go on to consider how they—in themselves machines for living in—may become parts of a still larger efficient mechanism which may help us to solve our problems of living. As we know, it is not only the purely mechanical problems which need to be solved.

2 3

1 *The Nottingham Playhouse at night.*
2 *Circulation areas. The aluminium mural can be seen on the right.*
3 *The auditorium.*
4 *The stage seen from the back of the auditorium.*

4

1 upper foyer
2 stair
3 lower foyer
4 balcony entrance
5 balcony
6 stalls
7 orchestra pit

8 upper stage
9 stage
10 fly gallery
11 fly tower
12 boiler house
13 open area
14 carpenter's shop

5

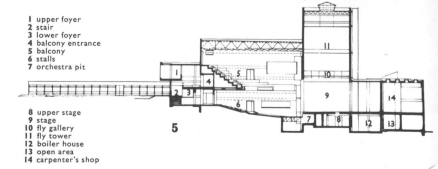

5　Town design

In earlier times the size of towns was dictated by the need for supply and defence. Too small a town was difficult to defend, as too few citizens were available to man the walls. If the town grew too large, defence became just as difficult, lines of communication were longer and the defenders could not be switched about quite so easily to meet surprise attacks. Stores had to be enormous to keep the inhabitants supplied during a siege. In peace time the town could not be so large as to outgrow the surrounding country's ability to produce food. But the industrial town, no longer restricted by such considerations, could expand almost indefinitely—and often did. During most of the last century hardly any control was exercised over the manner of this expansion, and towns grew in an abnormal fashion, like diseased organisms. It is therefore little wonder that many towns no longer discharge their functions efficiently.

Imagine a town which has grown up round a cross roads. Originally it was in harmony with its site, and the roads were sufficient to cater for its modest needs. Then industrialists added their installations on the outskirts. They did not want to build expensive new roads so they kept as close as possible to the existing ones. Industrial suburbs grew along the main arteries. They attracted large numbers of workers who had to be housed. The left-over space was therefore filled in with housing estates, vast, nightmarish built-up areas, neither town nor country, which became the accepted by-product of industrial towns. Industry and housing were not clearly defined territorially but intermixed so that streets of dwellings became access roads for industry and lorries thundered past within a few feet of living rooms. All the roads now had to carry an amount of traffic very much in excess of that for which they were designed, but usually there was no room for widening them because both sides were lined with factories and houses. Meanwhile the town centre, which now had to deal with the needs of a very much larger population, became overcrowded. The pressure on accommodation for business and administration in the town centre and the accompanying rise in ground values forced most people who lived there to move out. Their houses were taken over for offices and workshops that attracted a volume of traffic for which the streets were not designed. Smaller industries crept in as space became available, creating noise and dirt and further choking the streets with transport. The old layout of the town was no longer able to cope with the conditions which were now imposed upon it. From almost every point of view the town ceased to be the efficient mechanism it had once been.

1　**2**

4

5

6

7

A busy main road, **1**, with dwellings on one side, **2**, and industrial buildings on the other, **3**. Rochdale, a northern industrial town, **4**. Residential streets and industrial installations grew up in a haphazard manner; vast areas neglected by civic authorities and private individuals add to the picture of chaos. A London street, **5**, with housing sandwiched between warehouses and factories. **6** A small industrial workshop has crept into an unclaimed plot. Dreariness is now complete. **7** A railway bridge wedged between houses in London

The mechanical and visual chaos which confronts us today in most of our towns was not wholly created during the heyday, the free-for-all, of the Industrial Revolution. Much of it has been added in our own time, and is still being added in the same ill-considered, piecemeal manner. Few new houses serve their purpose as well as one would expect in a machine age; rarely are modern techniques of building fully exploited. The street, the neighbourhood, the traffic arteries are so often quite unrelated to the new developments. Land is used most illogically.

There are still many houses being built, whole neighbourhoods and shopping centres developed, which are amateurish in their basic approach to town design, derived from wishful thinking rather than from a strict analysis of conditions and needs. The proposal for the redevelopment of Piccadilly Circus in London, **1**, was made by a Royal Academician about the end of the Second World War—forty years after Garnier's plan, twenty years after Corbusier's plan! This Piccadilly plan still rests on the time-honoured idea of designing a façade first and then cramming everything necessary behind the façade. This is as out of place in the middle of a metropolis as a half-timbered façade on a nuclear reactor. Although this monstrosity was not allowed to come into the world, lesser miscreations are being perpetrated up and down the country, even today. Mock Georgian façades, screening off badly laid out, inconvenient, ill-lit offices, are still going up. Redevelopments of main thoroughfares where pedestrians and shoppers still have to take pot luck crossing the road are carried out. These are both aspects of the same unrealistic approach to town design. They solve no problems, but add to the difficulties of out-of-date environments by increasing the number of insoluble problems.

It is now being recognised that problems cannot be solved in isolation, that architecture must concern itself more and more with town design. If a truly well-designed building is to give of its best, it must be related to the whole environment and play its part as a cog in the machine which is the town. What good is a modern railway station if it is impossible to park nearby? Is it right to build rows of houses immediately adjoining a motorway? If modern buildings are to be really functional town design cannot be left to chance.

This is only one aspect of the problem; there are also social requirements. For instance, land is often developed in bits and pieces so that the best use is not made of it. Even bigger developments are often unrelated to social needs. Many of our most neglected areas in urgent need of renewal are not being redeveloped. Private developers cannot expect much profit from their investments in such

1

2

areas; local authorities have not the money to redevelop very much at once. At the same time a great deal of redevelopment is going on in places which do not, from a social point of view, require it, but offer rich rewards to speculators. Such a muddle-headed, lop-sided way of 'improving' our environment cannot work in the long run. Developments which are unrelated to physical needs (such as traffic) will create a lop-sided environment, those unrelated to social needs will create a lop-sided society.

2 *A new housing development but the only 'recreation' area is this traffic island from whose seats the inhabitants may watch the traffic milling round them.*
3 *A new office block.*
4 *New houses, but do they make the best use of the land in a fairly crowded neighbourhood?*
5 *Is this a town? The natural organism of earlier towns is gone and what we witness now is an abnormal growth, like a disease, eating ravenously into the helpless countryside. Soon the few remaining islands of fields and trees will be engulfed.*

3

4

5

The problem is so enormous, after generations of indifference, that one hardly knows where to begin. Yet beginnings can be and have been made. The Civic Trust, which was set up to carry out limited but comprehensive improvements, and to encourage people to take a greater interest in their surroundings, has achieved some remarkable results. Colour is used in such a way that the character of each building is enhanced and at the same the unity of the street picture preserved. Signs are simplified or redesigned, new street furniture introduced. In this way neglected areas have been given a new lease of life; once again it has become a pleasure to walk about in the streets, to shop, to gossip.

1 2

3

4

5

6

The central area of Burslem before improvement, 3. Shops, as they used to be, 1, and as they are now, 2. The drab neglected area in front of the town hall, 5, has become a pleasant corner, 6. This overall effect has been achieved by meticulous attention to every detail, 4.

With a little determination we could go much further. Picture **1** shows an average town square, a familiar sight in so many British towns. It is possible to argue that the items which clutter up this civic space are necessary for the functioning of the town. But by re-routing the traffic—which will in most cases also help to speed it up—many items become superfluous, **2**. The dead, unused space in the middle of the roundabout can be given to pedestrians, and several other changes can make it possible to see and experience the square as *space*, even though buildings have actually been added to it. If every town attacked its neglected areas in this way, people would become proud of their environment once more and take a more active part in determining its shape and appearance. And these things are possible, even without any vast rebuilding schemes.

When very old buildings have to be demolished because they are no longer safe or because they do not any longer conform with the living and working conditions which we expect, we should think very hard before deciding simply to erect new buildings on the ground plans of the old. In some cases re-building offers enormous opportunities of improving our environment. In few cases are these opportunities taken.

1

2

Architecture does not start with bricks and mortar, but with the needs of individuals and communities. Building must be preceded by processes of thought and of intuition which will determine its shape. For instance, in the case of a residential area, one of the first things to decide is the density of the new development. This will depend on a number of different considerations, including social ones, and will affect both the layout and the form of the buildings.

If the density is too low and buildings are consequently far apart, the general feeling of the neighbourhood will be too open; it will 'feel draughty'. Buildings will be too far apart to fall readily into relationships with each other. Closely spaced buildings and houses will, if properly designed, form definite spaces between them and harmonious relationships. One must also decide how many dwellings shall have their own private gardens, for this will determine the amount of space left over for communal purposes. Picture **4** shows a layout of buildings for a certain site in London designed for a density of 136 persons per acre. Most dwellings have private gardens and are contained in two- and three-storey houses. Picture **3** shows a layout for the same area with the same density, but this is designed for the maximum of open space and few private gardens. You can see that not only the layout of the buildings but also their shape, their architecture, will be affected by these social considerations. In our choice we shall be influenced by the importance we attach to private and to public space. We may also feel that with increased car ownership fewer people will be anxious to have their own gardens and will prefer to get away for their leisure. On the other hand, the facilities associated with universal car ownership —access roads, ramps, garages, hard-standing, etc. —become a heavy economic burden if they are not concentrated in a densely populated area. A fairly high density may therefore be both desirable and unavoidable. If we increase the density to 200 persons per acre, yet another layout will be called for and another form of building. **5**, **6**. Here is a series of dwellings linked by a pedestrian road at the level of the second floor. The road at ground floor level is for motor cars only and also provides parking space. Even a building of such complexity can be erected from pre-fabricated parts and there is no reason why it should not be visually stimulating. With its systems of circulation rather like those of a natural organism, this would indeed be an efficient machine for living in.

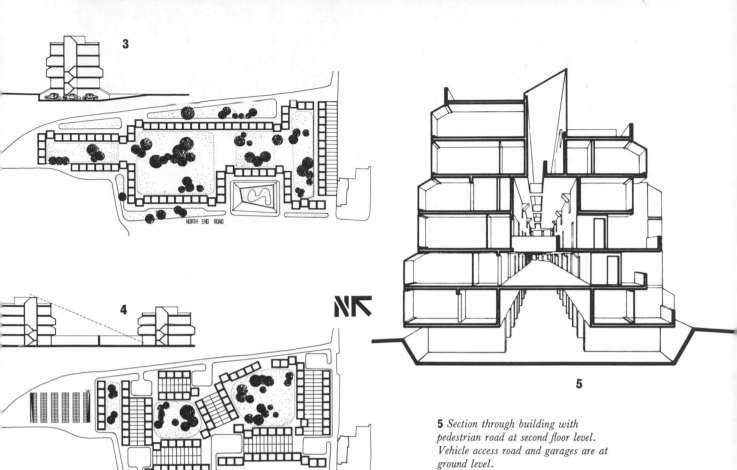

3

4

NORTH END ROAD

NORTH END ROAD

NⵏⲔ

5

5 *Section through building with pedestrian road at second floor level. Vehicle access road and garages are at ground level.*

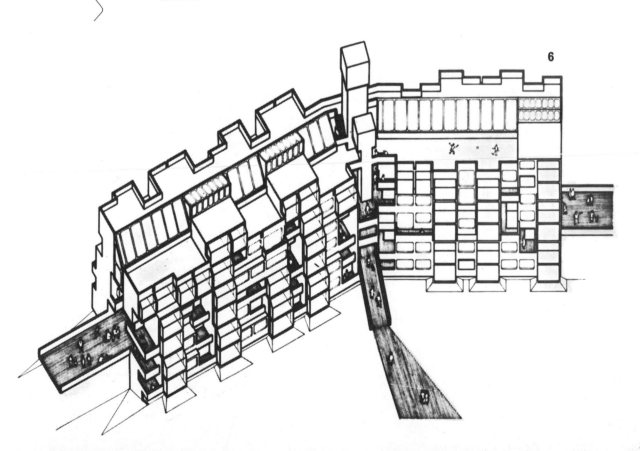

6

This is one of a great number of possible solutions for redeveloping a neighbourhood. Even so it is not the complete solution. Many other factors have to be considered in the preparation of such a design, especially when larger areas are involved. For instance, this design makes provision for access roads and parking but does not tackle the wider problems created by the mass-produced motor car. These are not new. In fact, traffic problems existed in large populated areas such as London as long ago as the turn of the century, **1**, but they were either by-passed or dealt with in an amateurish way.

It is only by studying the whole problem in great detail, by analysing it, that we are likely to arrive at a satisfactory answer. Most roads in use today follow the routes of roads laid down centuries ago. In the meantime industries and townships have sprung up, yet we are still forcing the old roads to serve our new conditions. To widen such existing roads is not the real answer. Picture **2** shows a map of Newbury, Berkshire, with its existing road system. The diagram, **3**, shows the visual representation of the results of a number of enquiries into the use of the roads. The arrows, called desire-lines, show the direction in which people would travel if they could drive as the crow flies, in other words, where the majority of people would want a road in order to travel by the shortest possible route. The bigger arrows indicate the greatest demand. It is clear that many people do not really want to go to the town centre at all, but have to pass through it because it lies on the only road to their destination. A new road system based on these and other findings would look rather like diagram **4**. Two main roads would by-pass the town centre to the north and the south. A secondary road would connect the two, with several smaller local roads branching out from it. The congestion in the town centre would be relieved, which would not only ease the flow of traffic, but would make conditions in the town much more pleasant. The market square could be made traffic-free altogether.

We must remember that this is only a plan; much would depend on how such a plan were carried out. It would have to be part of a redevelopment scheme, so that town and transport system were wholly integrated. Both could then be efficient in their own right. Such a plan would therefore give architects and civil engineers the opportunity to build houses and to create open civic space inside the built-up area, and roads and bridges in the country. These structures should be of such a design that they would not have to be excused as necessary evils, things we simply had to put up with whether we liked it or not, but valid twentieth-century additions to the townscape and landscape. When we look at such isolated examples

1

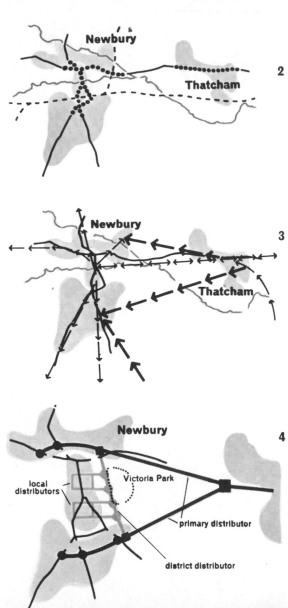

2

3

4

local distributors

Victoria Park

primary distributor

district distributor

as the Hammersmith flyover, **6**, and the bridge and junction of the M4 motorway, **5**, we realise that such solutions, like the great artistic solutions of past periods, add something significant to our environment. The Hammersmith flyover is more than a mere convenience, it is a visual symbol of our age with which we can identify ourselves. Such schemes, by looking far into the future, can ease many traffic problems in and around our towns for many years. Town centres, relieved of traffic which uses them as thoroughfares, may once again assume their proper function. But to do this properly we must build so that problems do not have a chance to arise; in other words, we must try to look at conditions as they may exist in twenty or thirty years' time.

6

1 *Traffic in London, 1900*
2 *The dotted lines indicate heavily overloaded roads. The grey patches are built-up areas.*
7 *A pedestrian precinct. Before such a scene can become a reality our traffic problems have to be attacked in a comprehensive way.*

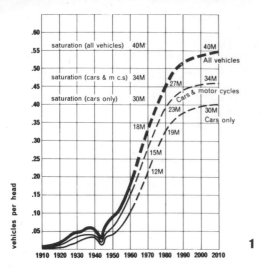

1

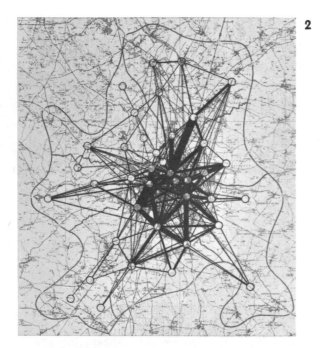

2

We know now that car ownership is increasing at an alarming rate, as shown by the graph, **1**, and unless we do something drastic about controlling the use of motor cars, they will saturate the towns and choke them to death. Most of us find the prospect of such control unacceptable. We believe that each person should be allowed to do as he pleases and we do not look kindly at regulations which will interfere with this freedom. So we build new roads, or extend existing ones, in the fond hope that by adding facilities in this hand-to-mouth way we shall keep out of trouble. How ludicrous this attitude is was demonstrated when a traffic census was taken in the city of Leicester with a view to devising an improved traffic system. Diagram **2** shows the desire-lines of the rush hour traffic in Leicester, the thickest lines indicating the densest traffic. After a great deal of research, including the use of computers, it was found that a diagram for 1995 would look as shown in **3**. The map of Leicester, **4**, shows what would have to be done to cope with this increased flow of traffic. New roads, some of them sixteen lanes wide, would have to be built. The junctions, **5**, would be extremely complex and therefore costly. In the centre of the town vast car silos would have to be built—motor age cathedrals—several storeys high and covering 133 acres. The intersections would swallow up another 48 acres. The shopping area would be reduced to the dark patch in diagram **4**. The environment would be destroyed and dehumanised. As the report states, 'This is the dilemma: the city centre or the motor car'.

3

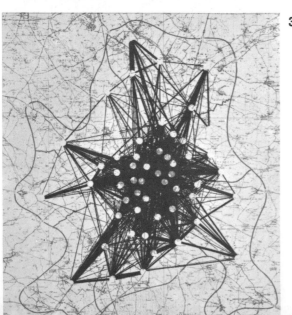

4

In devising a way out of this dilemma the planning officer was guided by two basic considerations: that the valuable parts of the existing environment should be safeguarded as far as possible, and that the motor car is both inefficient and, if used indiscriminately, antisocial. Diagram **6** shows a comparison of road space requirements for private cars and a bus, both streets carrying the same number of people. It is obvious that if a great number of private car users could be persuaded to use public transport it would considerably reduce the traffic difficulties, even with the present road system. This might be achieved by building interchange car parks at various points on the approach routes to the centre. Good bus services would then take the passengers to their destinations. This expedient would relieve the central roads of much traffic and consequently the new road system would not have to be so comprehensive as that for the unrestricted use of private transport. Only four to six lanes would be needed. The bus service would be carried on by three distinct types of vehicle, for express service, inter-district service, and city centre service; the latter would provide only standing accommodation in small vehicles. There

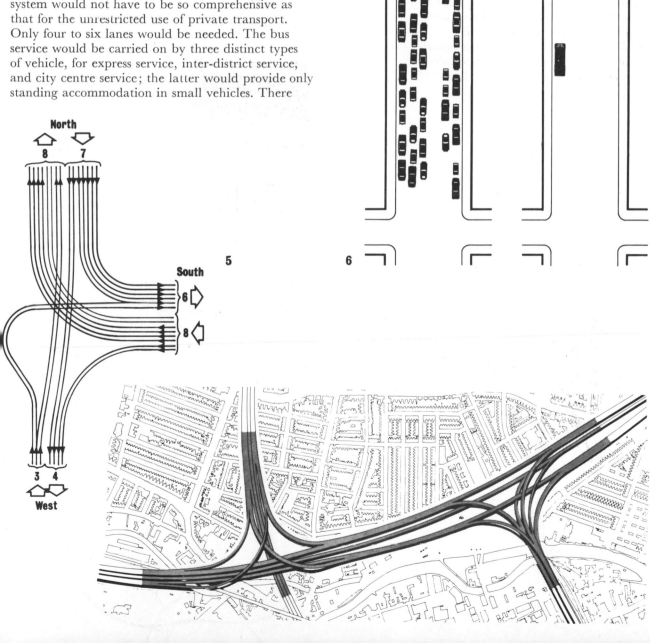

1·4 Passengers

At Peak Hours
Over 70
Passengers

North

8 7

South

5

6 ⇨

8 ⇦

6

3 4

West

would also be a monorail service. Pedestrian
conveyors or moving pavements could also be
considered as part of the plan. All the desirable
features of the town would be retained and roads
would be constructed to leave intact as many of
them as possible. The reduced volume of traffic
would make it possible to close certain roads to
traffic altogether and make them into pedestrian
precincts. This plan would have the advantage of
costing only a fraction of the plan for unrestricted
use of private transport. It would also mean that
the environment would not have to be destroyed,
but could be even significantly enriched.
The opportunities created by such planning for a
truly twentieth-century townscape are enormous.
The new roads in their new spatial settings would
create new experiences of townscape. The older
areas need not be disfigured; they too could be
incorporated in the overall design, with limited
motor access and great safe areas reserved wholly
for pedestrians. This can be done only by
comprehensive planning. Piecemeal development
can never solve any big problems, but will destroy
what little real town (and country) we have left.

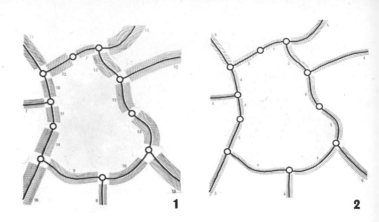

1

2

EXPRESS SERVICE

INTER DISTRICT SERVICE

CITY CENTRE SERVICE

3

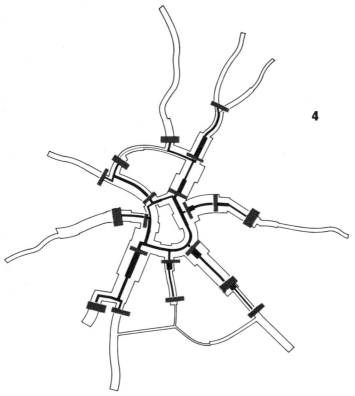

4

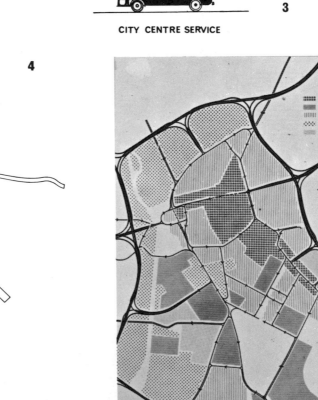

5

Road systems for indiscriminate use of private transport, **1**, and for restricted use, **2**.
3 Different types of buses for different purposes
4 Approach roads and their interchange car parks
5 Plan for Leicester, *1995*. Simplified road system; the town can now assume its proper function. Compare with **4**, page *128*.
6 The shopping centre with monorail, buses and escalator
7 Traffic-free areas with travelators
8 Proposal for redeveloping a London neighbourhood

Many of our largest towns are still growing and
becoming more and more unmanageable.
Redevelopments and improvements founder on the
sheer size of the problem. From time to time it
becomes necessary to start new towns to absorb the
increase in town population which hitherto has been
accommodated in the sprawling half-world on the
outer fringes of large towns.

The design of a new town considered as a living
organism and not simply as a number of houses
added together is a most complex and exacting
task. What in the past evolved over centuries
through the slow method of trial and error,
gradually adjusting itself to varying demands of
different periods and successive generations, must
now be designed in one operation, it must be
calculated, imagined and guessed at. A town
designer knows that any mistake in his design may
involve many people in a great deal of discomfort
and unhappiness. Here are a few of the things he
must think about and relate to each other.

First of all some basic considerations. If we compare
a town in the shape of a circle, **1**, to one designed
on an oval plan, **2**, one thing strikes us at once.
Since people should ideally be living within walking
distance of their town centre, the overall size of the
town will be determined by the walking distance
between centre and periphery. This should be not
more than about seven minutes. We can see from
the diagram that in an oval town the central area,
containing shops and offices, libraries and places
of entertainment, would serve a larger town area.
In either shape the maximum walking distance from
the centre is seven minutes. In the oval plan the
central area would be strung out instead of
concentrated in one blob. There are other
advantages in a long plan. Transport services which
would radiate from the centre in a round town, **3**,
would leave large areas unserved. In a long plan
a similar service would cover the town area much
more efficiently, **4**. Diagram **5** shows how a long
town plan may be served by roads which connect
it to trunk roads and so to other towns, a ring
road which serves internal needs, and from this,
short roads to the central area.

The next step is to decide on the type of housing.
But before this can be decided the designer must
know to what density he has to work. Here a
number of different ideas will occur to him. He
knows that apart from the central area there must
also be other smaller shopping centres, schools,
local libraries. Again each one of these can serve
only a certain area, **6**. In a town of low density
most people will have to walk long distances in
order to get to these points or will drive to them,
creating traffic and parking problems, whilst those
within its neighbourhood (shown by the circles)

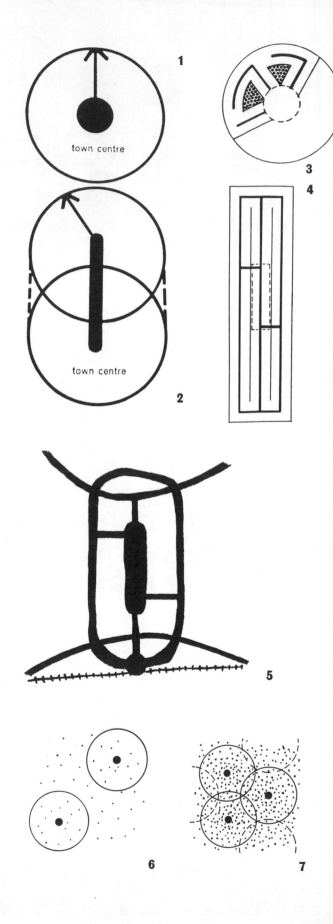

will have no choice. But in a densely populated town, **7**, it is possible for the areas served by these smaller centres to overlap, which not only reduces walking distances but also makes it possible for many people to choose between different shops, etc. Higher densities than have in recent times been thought desirable commend themselves from many points of view, at least for the central core of the town. From these and many other considerations our designer will perhaps draw up his first tentative layout of the new town, **8**. In it are shown the central high density area, surrounded by areas of lower densities, the industrial areas, and the system of communications.

This is the overall plan, but now the details of this plan must be thought about, for it is in those details that the plan will touch the individual citizen. Diagram **9** shows a possible method of linking groups of houses into a neighbourhood by means of a circular road which feeds each group. In this way it is possible to bring motor cars to each house and at the same time provide a safe area for pedestrians. Motor traffic and pedestrians would in fact approach each house and each group of houses by different routes. Suitably placed underpasses would enable a child to walk to school or to the nearest shop or bus stop without ever crossing a road.

These are standards which a civilised community should have built into its town, but they mean that streets and neighbourhoods would look quite different from those we are used to. If the appearance and construction of a street are to be changed, the town designer has the freedom not to place houses in a conventional relationship to the street but to arrange them in such a way that each house gets the maximum amount of sunlight, **10**, **11**.

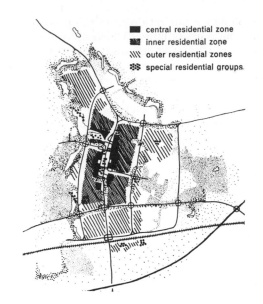

central residential zone
inner residential zone
outer residential zones
special residential groups.

8

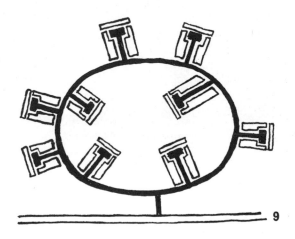

9

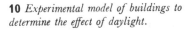

10 *Experimental model of buildings to determine the effect of daylight.*

10

11

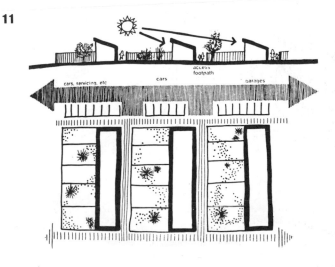

access
footpath

cars, servicing, etc
cars
garages

Now the designer can get down to the problem of designing the types of houses which are required, although details must be left until later. They may be built of prefabricated units, or of local materials or, preferably, of both. The designer can now determine the proportion of open space in relation to the built-up area, the height of the various types of housing for the different parts of the town, the type of car parking, and many other aspects.
Picture **1** shows a drawing with a suggested housing complex built for a density of 250 persons per acre; picture **2** shows houses for a density of 160. Car parks can be screened by trees and shrubs, **3**, to do away with the usual unsightly expanse of parked cars.

The town centre would be constructed on entirely different principles from residential areas. Most town designers now think of town centres as built up in several layers in order to concentrate them in a comparatively small area instead of letting them 'sprawl'. Our designer must think of providing space for shops and municipal offices, cafés and restaurants, service roads for the shops which do not interfere with the pedestrian precincts, other roads and car parks, and probably an independent public transport system, perhaps in the form of a monorail. He is designing a machine for the use of a community. It will look like an efficient machine, **5**, and because it is a machine for human use all the working parts must conform to the physical as well as emotional needs of human beings. In a properly designed and organised town centre, laid out at several levels, there should be everything that human beings need to feel at peace with themselves as well as with the world around them. It should be stimulating and should give them a feeling of belonging to something bigger than themselves.

Such designs, if they are to be really efficient, cannot, as we have seen, be achieved without a great deal of creative thought and imagination, but they also require a great deal of research into many aspects of the town's life. For instance, two independent traffic systems, one for motor traffic and one for pedestrians, **7**, must be incorporated into the design of the town. Desire-line diagrams for different times of the day will give the designer a good idea of the kind of road network required. This in turn will have to be adjusted to suit the nature of the ground and the layout of the housing, which will in turn be dependent on the road network.

Our designer will also have to investigate what sort of people will inhabit the new town. The cross section of the population of a new town will differ from that of the rest of the country in several important respects. More younger couples are likely to be attracted to a new town, so that more schools will be required than for a town of similar size elsewhere. This in turn will affect the layout of the individual neighbourhoods.

Finally, the designer will know that it is impossible to build a whole new town in one operation. A start will have to be made with one part of the plan and this area will then have to be enlarged over ten or twenty years. The plan must therefore be adaptable to this planned growth; at each stage it should be a more or less complete unit, which can function efficiently and in which people can live happy lives, even though it has not yet reached its ultimate size. All the requirements of a well-designed town must apply to each stage as well as to the finished town. We can see that this requires an organic design of unbelievable complexity.

1

2

3

4

5

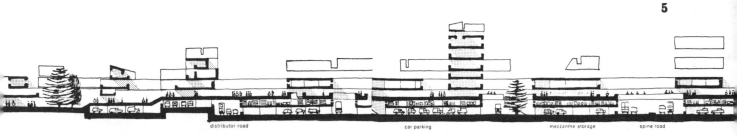

distributor road   car parking   mezzanine storage   spine road

7 *shows pedestrian areas and vehicle access roads interlinked in one intricate pattern.* **6** *is a detail of such a pattern, a neighbourhood in whose layout traffic segregation and light have been studied.*

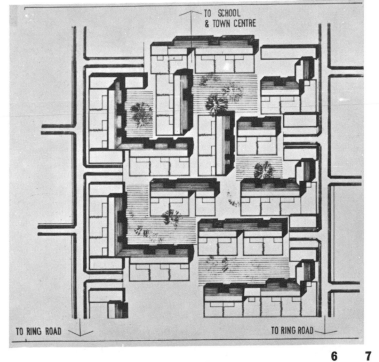

6   7

6 Building for the future

Existing towns have grown up over centuries and even millenia, during which time successive generations have added ideas and methods to those they inherited from their forefathers. In this slow evolution they unconsciously gave expression not only to their material needs, in the construction of houses and the layout and composition of streets, but also to certain spiritual and emotional demands. These not only influenced the solutions of larger issues and material problems but also the *manner* in which they were carried out and related: the many details of townscape which determined the quality of a town, its peculiar flavour, character or charm.

These details vary from town to town because of local conditions—materials, climate, industry, etc.—and from age to age because different values loom large in men's minds. The quality of a town results from these details which arouse the sense of elation or of dejection we experience when we walk through the streets and squares of a town, or when we come to live in it.

Apart from withholding the view and so increasing its effect when we do eventually attain it, this design also creates a pleasantly shaped piazza on the left, **4**, **8**. At the far end of the irregular open space a narrow lane connects with another street. On the face of it there is nothing noteworthy about it, but on investigation it reveals subtleties. As everywhere in Bath, harmonising curves are evident: the curvature of the line of the posts which mark this as a pedestrian area is matched by the curvature of the side of the first house and the backs of some of the other houses. On walking to the other end of the piazza we notice that another row of similar posts encloses an access street to the terrace just beyond, **5**. The lane which we noticed from the other side of the piazza can now be seen to descend under some trees to a lower level with the different levels linked by stairs, **6**, **7**. The way in which the different levels are managed, with the shady lane sloping away, suggests a craftsmanlike appreciation of what conditions had to offer. It could not have been designed like this by a town planner at his drawing table; it must have been devised on the spot by someone who had a sense for the genius of the place.

1

2

3

The curved approach to the Circus in Bath must have been designed for its visual effect. At first a full view of the Circus is withheld, owing to the curved street, **1**, but as we get closer to it a more general view comes into the picture, **2**. **3** Had we approached this important part of the townscape of Bath by a straight road, we should have seen it from far off and it would have remained in view all the time until we reached it, by which time the visual experience would have become stale.

4

5

7

8

At the end of the main shopping street of Loreto, in Italy, there is a break spanned by an arch, **3**, between the otherwise continuous front of houses. Beyond, we see a number of houses at a lower level, we cannot see the ground on which they stand. In a sense this is a visual half-statement: the houses are stated, but not how they connect to the ground and so to the part of the ground on which we happen to be standing. A half-statement like this has the tendency of making us want to find out about the other half. We are therefore induced to explore this part and made to approach it with a sense of anticipation. On the other side of the same street a similar break between the houses occurs; a stairway leads down from it and disappears round the corner, **1**. We see a section of the distant landscape between the houses. Here again a number of questions suggest themselves: where does the stairway lead to? What is the landscape like to the left and right of the small sample which is shown? These views have important effects on our minds, for we are given incentives to explore the town, to relate the different parts to each other and to the countryside surrounding it. At the other end of the street is the main square with the church, **2**. The transition from the narrow intimate street to the wide open square is gradual: the street broadens out into a funnel-like opening so that we pass from the narrow enclosure of the street into the open square with its grandiose façades without any sense of suddenness. This gradual change is further accentuated by the fact that we approach the church—the centrepiece of the town—from an angle. We do not get the full visual impact of the façade of the church until we are well into the middle of the square, **4**.

1

2

3

4

A house built next to the cathedral of Perugia made use of the arcade which projects beyond the actual structure of the cathedral, **5**. The two buildings are now integrated to an extent not often to be met with. They hug each other, with obvious effects on the townscape. It is difficult to see how neighbourliness could be taken further.

The rich textures of a corner in Pavia, **6**, would in themselves contribute enough visual interest to make this part pleasant to walk through. But the very large stones which form part of the wall on the left dramatise the corner in a most unexpected way. It may be that part of an old wall was left standing when this house was put up, or perhaps some old stones were used from an old building which made room for the new one. This effect, like those of the preceding examples, could not have been worked out in the designer's mind. They come about as a matter of course when man uses his sensitivity to his environment, to the materials he uses and to the purposes for which he makes things. It cannot be done by planning only. The different stone textures and patterns cannot be explained or justified in cold words but only by the visual and sensuous experience which we derive from them. And ultimately it is this feeling which can only be obtained through one's senses which makes buildings accessible to the human spirit, and gives meaning to the larger spatial relationships.

6

5

In the last chapter we discussed a few of the current ideas on town design which must replace the haphazard methods of building our environment which have been in force until now. These ideas are not in any way extreme but form a minimum requirement for a modern town from which further —and more advanced—ideas can be developed. If they were adopted in their entirety they would give our towns a vastly different appearance. Nevertheless, they would still not guarantee us the towns we require, for they are only plans, and everything would depend on the manner in which these plans were realised.

Some of these considerations may seem too trifling for a town designer who deals with large masses and movements and spaces. He may not realise from a look at his drawings that a certain building will obliterate a certain landmark, or look gross in relation to it. He may not notice that a certain corner in his town will be little used, through its particular position, and so become 'dead' space. He may be unaware of the potentialities of particular materials and other, lesser, details which can be decided only by an intimate knowledge of local conditions and a feeling for the genius of the place. When we look at what has been done in town design in recent years, we must judge these achievements not only with an eye on mechanical efficiency but also with our senses attuned to the manner in which this efficiency has been achieved. In the sadder cases of town development, we must be aware of the price at which this efficiency has been bought. It is in such ways that we must seek the sensuous and emotional meaning to town design.

The Park Hill Housing estate in Sheffield, **2,** is one of the most significant developments in large scale housing in recent years; it must form the model for many another scheme which strives to do the same thing. This has for some time been a real slum area and although attempts to improve it have been made in the past, they have never had sufficient scope and power to make any sizeable inroads into the problem. The new development appears at first sight to be a series of buildings; it is in fact a single building with three distinct junctions between its component wings. It stands on a sloping site so that the height of the building varies between four storeys at the highest point of the site and fourteen at the lowest. There are lifts and stairs for vertical communication and decks for horizontal communication.

These decks are not be to compared to the corridor balconies so often seen in other types of housing. They are wide enough for tradesmen to deliver their goods or for furniture to be moved by specially constructed trolleys, for children to play in and for adults to meet and gossip. All the front doors open on to the deck and any point can be reached from any other on the same level without descending and going up again. They are to all intents and purposes streets—the name 'street deck' is justified—but without the inherent danger of fast-moving traffic. Because of the sloping nature of the site and the fact that all the street decks are horizontal, some run out to ground level at different points, but the higher ones run the full course of the whole building. Since south and west aspects have as far as possible been reserved for living rooms, the street deck must change its position within the structure of the building, as the direction of the building changes. In the diagram, **5,** the layout of the building is shown, and the street deck is also indicated. It will be seen that at certain points the street deck crosses over to the other side. It would be impossible to decide which is the façade, if such an expression still carries any meaning.

To make available a wide variety of accommodation both maisonettes and flats are incorporated in the design. The diagram, **3,** shows how they are related to the deck.

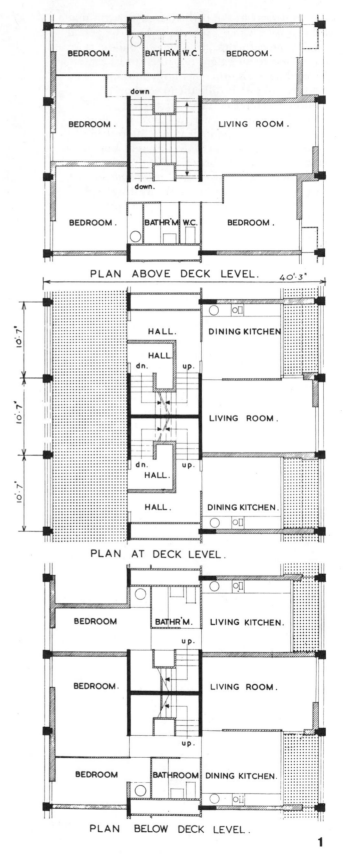

PLAN ABOVE DECK LEVEL. 40'.3"

PLAN AT DECK LEVEL.

PLAN BELOW DECK LEVEL.

1 *shows the different types of accommodation at different levels,*
3 *is a section through three levels.* **4** *shows a corner unit.*

1

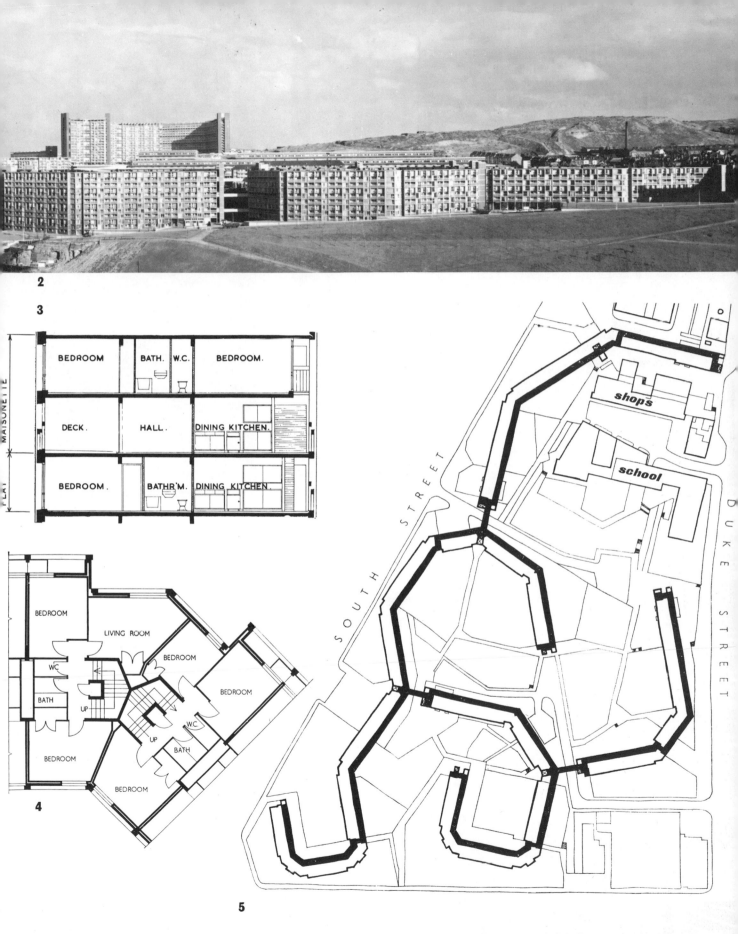

2

3

MAISONETTE

| BEDROOM | BATH. | W.C. | BEDROOM. |

| DECK. | HALL. | DINING KITCHEN. |

FLAT

| BEDROOM. | BATHR'M. | DINING KITCHEN. |

4

BEDROOM

LIVING ROOM

W.C.

BEDROOM

BATH

BEDROOM

UP

W.C.

UP

BEDROOM

BATH

BEDROOM

5

S O U T H   S T R E E T

D U K E   S T R E E T

shops

school

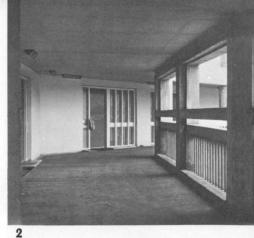

1 2

3

4

At the three junctions mentioned before, the decks
provide the only links between the different parts;
the building itself stops short of the junction. This
is to make room for a road to pass underneath, but
the general openness establishes a visual link
between the enclosed spaces which can be
appreciated even from the higher levels, **1**.
Purely visual elements have also entered into the
shaping of this functional-looking building. Without
the gaps at the junctions the enclosed spaces would
have given a greater feeling of isolation; as it is,
the spaces beyond can be seen and anticipated.
They become part of the whole scheme through an
act of visual unification. The heaviness of the
building itself is visually lightened by the gaps.
The points where the deck traverses the building to
change sides serve a similar purpose, for here again
the mass of the building is pierced to reveal the
space beyond, **3**. Seen from the outside the recessed
balconies with their pre-cast balusters and the open
decks provide a pattern of hollow forms, voids,
which contrast with the solid building, **4**. The
structural members are exposed everywhere and jut
out to enrich the walls with their three-dimensional

5

6

pattern. As one walks along the deck the view
constantly changes, **2**; sometimes only the interior,
enclosed, spaces are visible; at other times the
outside space only, or both at the same time. But
all these visual considerations have a functional
justification and chief amongst these is the need to
provide a good system of circulation. It is this which
adds the most dramatic feature to this vast building,
especially at the junctions, where the lift shafts
(vertical movement), with their cantilevered heads,
meet the decks (horizontal movement) in a spatially
exciting way. External staircases and access ramps
complete the picture of circulation, **5**, **6**.

1. *St James's as it used to be in the 18th century. During the following century large buildings which completely destroyed its character were added to the street. The Economist group, and especially the bank which faces the street, attempts to restore the original roofline. The open space between the buildings can be seen in the drawing, **2**. The relationship between completely open space and colonnades is shown in the diagram, **3**. Access to the piazza is provided by a ramp and stairs, **4**. In **5** the sculpture is seen full face against the side of an adjacent building. On page 146 further views of this intriguing piazza are shown. In all the pictures glimpses of the buildings and streets which surround the group can be seen through the gaps. Space is in a state of flux. In picture **3**, page 146, the interior of a building (foreground, left) the inner space of the colonnade, the central space of the piazza, and the outer space of the surrounding neighbourhood are combined in one overall conception of space.*

Where new buildings are added to an existing street the problem of matching the existing townscape always arises. But it is not necessary to clothe modern buildings in period costume in order to harmonise them with the rest of the street. In any case, most of our existing architecture and townscape is so inferior that to match it would invariably mean a lowering of standards. But this does not mean that the architect or town planner should not consider the character of the street or neighbourhood, The group of buildings in St. James's Street, London, illustrated on these pages shows how an architect may express the language of modern architecture, the needs of the modern town and yet not conflict with the interests of the existing townscape.

The largest of these buildings houses the offices of The Economist—a periodical—and the whole group is therefore referred to as the Economist group. The next smaller building is residential. The smallest is a bank. This latter building is in keeping with the scale of the other houses in the street so that its character remains unimpaired. The higher buildings are set back. They are not identical in appearance. The bank occupies the upper floors only of the bank buildings while the ground floor is a shop. The main banking hall therefore is the most important part of this building and this is expressed by the very much larger windows of this floor, the first. Historically speaking, this also corresponds to

the 'piano nobile' of Italian Renaissance palaces, which is imitated in many of the surrounding older buildings. The bay window which has been added to the older building on the left also has this characteristic. The high building which houses The Economist does not have a loftier first floor as this would not have been justified on either environmental or functional grounds. The residential building is a scaled down version of the Economist building; it has fewer storeys and the bays are only half the width. We can notice then several relationships which have been established between the different buildings of this complex. The scale and the important first floor windows tie the bank building to the street in general and through the new bay window of the older building to its immediate older neighbour. The large Economist building and the residential block are very similar and distinguished externally mainly by scale. The similar structure of the four elements provides the overriding unification. Inside the complex, a space has been created between these elements which further unifies the group through spatial relationships. These cannot be explained in so many words but must be experienced to be understood. These pictures show a few of them. The open ground floor colonnades allow the paved piazza to be extended under the outer walls of the buildings and even to invade the interior spaces of the large block. The views from

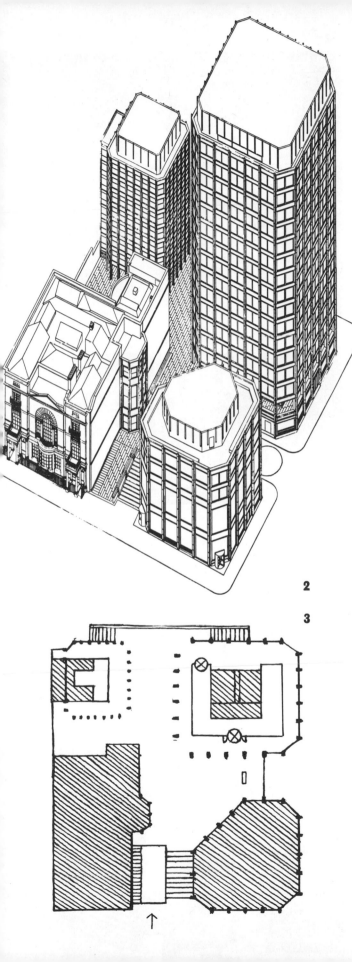

almost any point of the piazza give spatial perspectives which unify the group and show the larger space outside the piazza. The facings are of Portland stone and add a pleasantly coarse texture to the otherwise precise structures. The upright facings are kept off the ground—there can be no mistaking them for structural elements. All the balusters are of the same material. The sculpture is a perfect foil to its setting.

This group of buildings is not only good design as such; it goes much further and establishes links between inside and outside through devices which were demanded by the function of the buildings and which also make sense visually. We have already noted the dimensions of the banking hall windows as such an example. The chamfered corners of the office buildings are another. They were required in this form because of the particular office organisation for which they were built and because more light can be admitted in this form. They also make a more pleasantly shaped space between the buildings and add a further unifying element.

2

3

4

5

1

2

3

4

6

5

1–5 *Several views of the Economist group*

The development round St. Paul's, in London, consists largely of office blocks whose size has been carefully related to the cathedral and so designed as to enclose a number of pleasantly proportioned spaces for pedestrian use. The Paternoster development is a part of this scheme. As these pictures show, it too is a series of interconnected spaces with shops and cafés. Because of their varying size and treatment they give different spatial experiences, from tight enclosure to open space. The restrained architecture provides a good setting for the north side and cupola of St. Paul's. At night the floodlit cupola can be seen hovering beyond Paternoster Square in its Baroque magnificence, **8**.

6 *Model of Paternoster development*
7 *A shopfront in one of the smaller spaces*

7

8

1

2

3

4

5

6

7

8

New Towns have the advantage of comparatively few restrictions to contend with, far fewer than those imposed on developments in existing towns. Designers have in many cases been able to take advantage of those features of the countryside which in the past would have been suppressed if commercial demands conflicted with them. They have been able to allocate areas to the various services of a 20th century town where these would most readily fit into the rest of the pattern. They have also been able to create environments which are essentially humane and convenient in use. In most cases New Towns are based on a central core, radial roads connecting with a ring road, and a spur road connecting the ring road with a main road or motor way. Residential neighbourhoods are placed between the radial roads, each with its own community centre. The plan of Crawley shows these important features. The industrial area is to the north of the town; its position gives easy access to the railway, the ring road and the proposed motor way. Four neighbourhoods are inside the ring road, five outside it. At three points farmland stretches right up to the ring road and there are three parks within it.

The main square is a pedestrian precinct, but cars can gain access on one side. It is a wide spacious area, **1**, with trees and flower tubs dotted about. The pattern of the flagstones also enriches the scene. Although we can take it in as one huge space, it is full of small touches which induce people to use it as a civic space, in a way which most of us have never experienced. It is possible after shopping to rest under a shady tree, **2**, or in a recess amongst the bushes, **7**, to chat with friends, **3**, or to stroll around in the shopping streets, **4**, which lead off the square. The bandstand from the old Gatwick racecourse, **6** (seen in this picture against the other end of the square) is the only old object in the square; it contrasts pleasantly with the modern architecture, **5**. At the other end both planning and architecture become much more ordinary, **8**. Here vehicles and pedestrians have to fight it out once more.

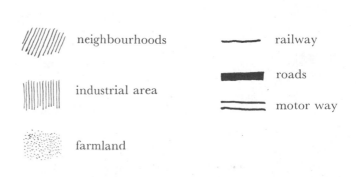

neighbourhoods	railway
industrial area	roads
farmland	motor way

The main square of Stevenage is even more complex. It is dominated by a clocktower, **1**, and, at the other end, by a raised platform, **4**, from which views of the square, such as **2**, may be obtained. Trees and shrubs soften the angularity of the architecture and the layout. The canopies over the shop fronts provide protection from the weather; it is also possible to cross from one side to the other under cover, **5**. Note also the different patterns and textures of the cobbles and flagstones, **2**, **6**. The various items of street furniture: seats, lamps, litter baskets, cycle stands, etc., are not only well designed in themselves; they are also related to each other by their positioning. Even the gutter, **7**, is carefully detailed. There are stimulating views in all directions. This civic area, unlike the one in Crawley, is wholly for pedestrians; there are car parks behind the shops and we can see some cars through an opening in a building, **8**. The plan shows the extent of the pedestrian area.

1

2

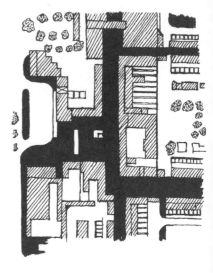

3

4

5

6

7

8

1

2

3

The main purpose of new developments is to replace an out-of-date environment which grew up haphazardly by one which is better related to human requirements of the present day. We have seen that, although this need not entail the destruction of the old, where a completely fresh start can be made we are free to impose on our new environment the stamp of the 20th century. By employing new building techniques, instead of imitating the ways of the past, we can create townscapes which breathe the very air of our own time, which solve many urgent problems of urban living in the language of the 20th century. In the best of the new schemes a unique quality of townscape has been created which is as natural to us now as the squares of Bloomsbury were to the Georgian era. The buildings in picture **1**, in Coventry and **2**, in Roehampton, London, have a boldness and excitement which mark them as truly of our day. Only the timid among us would want to forego this stimulus and shelter in the superficial cosiness of the familiar styles of the past. The possibilities of these developments are limitless. The model of the new centre of Cumbernauld, **4**, with its multi-level shopping and residential blocks linked by different lines of communication is one of the most exciting town schemes now being constructed. It can be seen as a delicate, sensitive instrument, in keeping with the subtle complexity of modern society.

In many new developments builders have been allowed to build houses which imitate the modern visual language without fully understanding it. New environments have been created which are both inefficient and visually incoherent although superficially 'modern'. But the most recent developments in the New Towns include residential neighbourhoods which are both efficient and humane. For instance, the vehicle access road in Cumbernauld, **5**, is a part of the overall plan which makes the whole town safe to pedestrians. It is here given visual expression by its purposeful, crisp detailing. In the old days this feature might have been considered less important than the front of the houses and less care expended on it, but here it is recognised as a vital part of the total environment. Likewise the house in Peterlee, **3**, has been designed not only as an efficient machine, but also as a visually significant one. We must always try to remember the underlying purpose: to create a humane environment, with the emphasis on humane, **6**.

4

5

6

In the last two chapters we have examined some of the new ideas on town building and designing. Achievements so far, when related to the size of the problem and its urgency, are still far from impressive. Good developments are still too few, and for each of these there are several dubious ones which are not real improvements at all. In the meantime the difficult living and working conditions in most large towns continue. These conditions are not in any way peculiar to Great Britain but are evident in Los Angeles as much as in Tokyo. Spurred by impatience, many young architects the world over have put forward new plans for towns designed for modern living conditions. All are agreed that something new is required, that the old ideas must be replaced by new ones giving expression to new beliefs, new needs, new thoughts, new feelings. They do vary, however, in the emphasis they place on these qualities. Let us look at two such plans which are entirely different and in many ways represent the two extremes of trends in modern town design.

The diagram, **1**, shows a diagrammatic representation of a new town which is based on the following assumptions. Modern conditions make it necessary for people to move house much more frequently than they used to. To provide an efficient environment for a society in a constant state of flux it is necessary to break completely with the historic traditions of town culture, which are now irrelevant. Their place must be taken by the most up-to-date technological and organisational knowledge. Since research in all branches of science and technology makes all industrial products obsolete in a short period of time, the elements of the modern town must be built for obsolescence, that is to say, they can be used up, disposed of and replaced. This will ensure a permanently changing, up-to-date, efficient environment. The desirability of a flexible organisation calls for structures which can be assembled to suit conditions at any time.

Tall towers would act as car silos and also as central supports for a cantilevered platform on which prefabricated dwellings could be placed. Permanently fixed cranes would hoist them up or lower them when they were no longer required. It would mean that any new inhabitants would not have to look for a house, but simply plug in to an existing system. This idea of a modern town has been given the name Plug-in-City. In the town centre a grid-like structure would hold together the different parts, its hollow members acting as transport channels for passengers and goods.

The drawing, **2**, should not be taken too literally, for it is only a plan without any of the details by which it should be judged. Much would depend on how such a plan lent itself to the adaptations and variations which human beings demand. This could

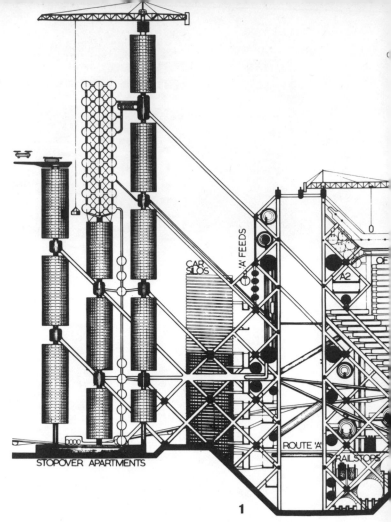

1

be the beginning of a tremendously exciting new phase in the evolution of the town, but one must wonder whether this excitement will not be short-lived, rather like one's pleasure in a new gadget, which soon fades when the newness has worn off. Perhaps in a world which consists of so many consumable items, which disappear after a short period of use, to be supplanted by more modern equipment, we should have at least some more permanent items to provide an element of stability. But even if we were not to accept this plan—and similar ones—in its entirety, there are many excellent ideas in it which should certainly be considered.

1 *Section through one of the busier parts of Plug-In City. Some of the dwellings on the housing towers look inward on to an open green space.*
2 *Another part of Plug-In City*
3, **4** *Several details*

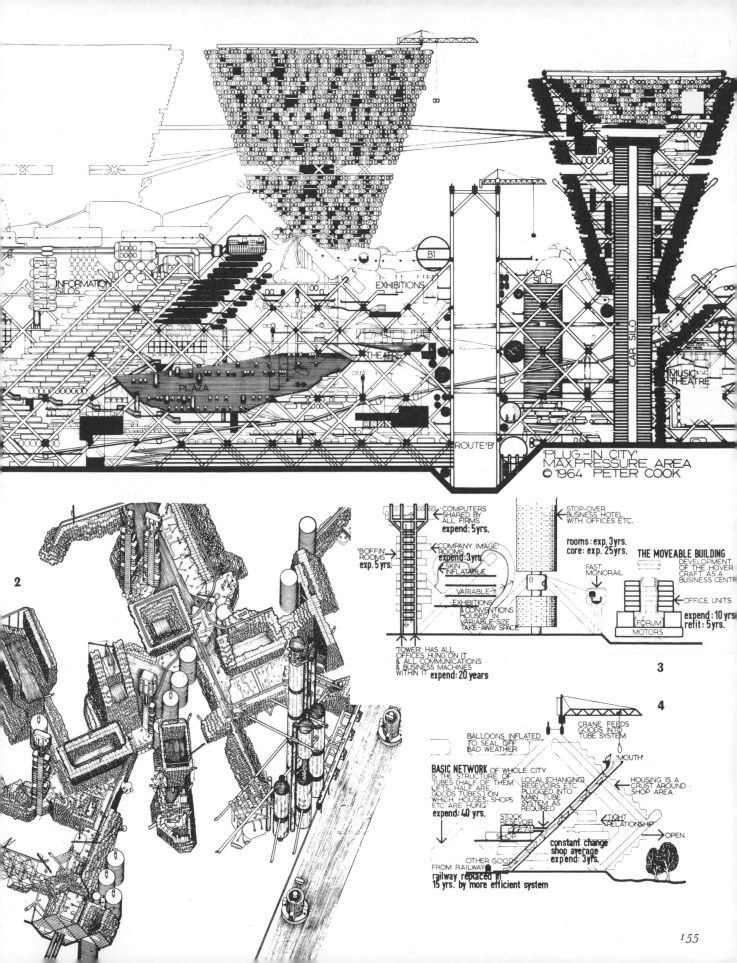

PLUG-IN CITY'
MAX.PRESSURE AREA
© 1964 PETER COOK

INFORMATION SILOS

EXHIBITIONS

CAR SILO

CAR SILO

PLAZA

THEATRE

ROUTE 'B'

B1

MUSIC THEATRE

2

3

COMPUTERS SHARED BY ALL FIRMS
expend: 5yrs.

STOP-OVER BUSINESS HOTEL WITH OFFICES ETC.

'BOFFIN' ROOMS exp. 5yrs.

'COMPANY IMAGE' ROOMS expend: 3yrs.

SKIN INFLATABLE

VARIABLE

rooms: exp. 3yrs.
core: exp. 25yrs.

FAST MONORAIL

THE MOVEABLE BUILDING
DEVELOPMENT OF THE HOVER CRAFT AS A BUSINESS CENTRE

EXHIBITIONS & CONVENTIONS HOUSED IN VARIABLE-SIZE TAKE-AWAY SPACE

OFFICE UNITS

expend: 10 yrs.
refit: 5yrs.

FORUM

MOTORS

'TOWER' HAS ALL OFFICES HUNG ON IT & ALL COMMUNICATIONS & BUSINESS MACHINES WITHIN IT expend: 20 years

4

BALLOONS INFLATED TO SEAL OFF BAD WEATHER

CRANE FEEDS GOODS INTO TUBE SYSTEM

'MOUTH'

BASIC NETWORK OF WHOLE CITY
IS THE STRUCTURE OF TUBES (HALF OF THEM LIFTS, HALF ARE GOODS TUBES) ON WHICH, HOUSES, SHOPS ETC. ARE HUNG'
expend: 40 yrs.

LOCAL (CHANGING) RESEVOIRS ETC. PLUGGED INTO MAIN TUBE SYSTEM AS REQUIRED

HOUSING IS A CRUST AROUND SHOP AREA

STOCK RESEVOIR

SHOP

TIGHT RELATIONSHIP

OPEN

constant change shop average expend: 3yrs.

OTHER GOODS FROM RAILWAY
railway replaced in 15 yrs. by more efficient system

Another one of the many new ideas for towns to be built in the future is the circular linear town proposed by Gordon Cullen. Briefly, it rests on the following principles. Our present-day towns have to accommodate movement of two different time scales—or speeds, for simplicity—traffic and pedestrians. Much of the chaos of modern towns is due to the indiscriminate mixing of these two. But if they could be separated, more efficient movement and more pleasant living conditions would result. Several ways of achieving this have already been discussed; another would be to allocate one through road to vehicular traffic with footpaths running at right angles to it, like spines, so that the two kinds of human locomotion do not have to get in each other's way. If a town were organised on this traffic-pedestrian system, it could therefore be very long indeed, as the long dimension would be covered by car or monorail, but its width would be determined by the pedestrian time scale, let us say 10-15 minutes' walk. If furthermore the long line formed by the road were closed into a circle, this would have many advantages, chief amongst them the fact that the relationship between town and country could be a very intimate one without spoiling the country, and giving each inhabitant easy access to it. The basic idea could be adjusted to meet the demands of different localities: the circle could be adjusted to the contours of the land and natural features found on it. It could even take in existing buildings and villages.

The plan of an existing area, **1**, and its possible development as a circular linear town, **8**, shows how this might be done. In this town it is possible to get from any point to any other point within 30 minutes' combined walking and travelling time. Nowhere is the country more than a few minutes' walk away. Instead of clustering town centre, utilities and housing together they are now strung out, connected by a circular through road and a noiseless monorail. Here are a few aspects of this new idea of town design.

The town centre would contain not only offices and the main shopping centre, but also places of entertainment, clubs, churches, institutes of adult education and cafés grouped together. Given appropriate architectural treatment, such a group could be stimulating to be in. There would be interesting views and perspectives, both inside and out. Instead of being surrounded by acres of built-up area this town centre would have direct access to the country, in this case the lake. Some high density housing would be part of the centre, and there would be more of it further along the road. Medium density housing would be placed at several points of the ring. Although industry would be confined to its own zone, certain light industries and crafts could be combined with other buildings such as

schools, clinics, shops and meeting places, giving some of the town's districts a distinct character, and providing employment for those who do not wish to or cannot travel to the industrial zone. The parkland in the middle of the town would become a huge village green. It would contain, apart from footpaths, a sports arena, a swimming pool and facilities for fishing and boating.

One of the main difficulties in designing housing in a new town is that a great variety of accommodation must be provided for many different needs which may change almost from year to year. But modern building methods should give us the possibility of building adaptable houses, so that they may be used in almost limitless ways and combinations. The diagram shows one such layout with its possible uses. In **2** the accommodation is occupied by a family with 2 children, the husband's or wife's parents and one room is used as a guest room, or bed-sitter. In diagram **3** the old people have died and a young couple have moved in. The accommodation is now organised as two separate flats. When they in turn have children the guest room can be annexed to their flat, **4**, and used as the children's bedroom. When the original family move out the second family's old folk can move in and the children's accommodation made into a bed-sitting room, **5**. There are of course many other possibilities. Housing difficulties are an important reason for people moving to other towns. By making housing adaptable we can help to keep a community together, with their local interests and traditions. Architecture and town design can then do more than merely give us civic spaces. They can also give us living conditions which so delight us that we are proud of them and become attached to them. Town design can also help us to solve many social problems which demand an architectural solution. If the town is to remain a living organism it must do all these things.

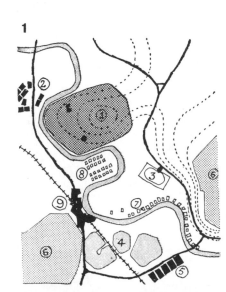

1

① OLD WOODED ESTATE SOLD FOR DEVELOPMENT
② INDUSTRY IN OLD ARMY HUTS
③ STOCK CAR RACING
④ INDUSTRIAL WORKINGS (GRAVEL PITS)
⑤ TRADING ESTATE
⑥ AREA SCHEDULED FOR OVERSPILL HOUSING
⑦ RIVERSIDE SHACKS & BUNGALOWS
⑧ CARAVANS
⑨ EXISTING VILLAGE

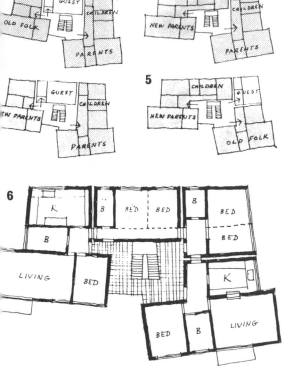

6 Basic lay-out of accommodation
7 Pedestrian way in the shopping area. The main road can be seen outside on the right.

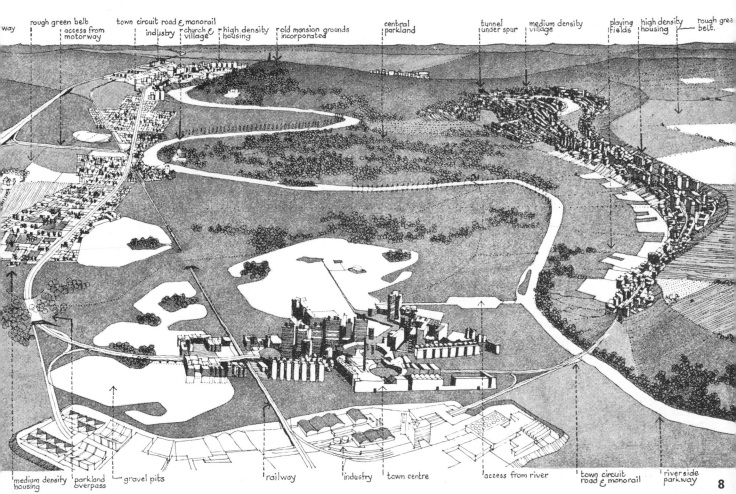

We have seen that each age of town building and town designing had its own peculiar character. It was not cast in an arbitrary form but represented the forces and ideas which were current at the time. The medieval town had its outstanding character of humanity and a craftsmanlike honesty of purpose. In essence it was turned in on itself. The Renaissance town looked outwards; it expressed the greater feeling for reality and the urge to explore nature and the world at large. The Baroque town expressed the grand gesture and the idea of the Grand Design. The modern town attempts to combine modern social attitudes and technological resources and the emotions they evoke.

These developments were paralleled by a widening of people's consciousness of *space as such*. Medieval man had no clear conception of space; things grew under his hand in a natural, organic way without his understanding clearly their relationship in space. Renaissance man, because he began to understand reality, was forced to explore it. He discovered the spatial relationships between individual objects in three-dimensional reality; without an understanding of these reality cannot be grasped. But even so, during the Renaissance only finite space could be comprehended, that is to say space enclosed by objects and limited by them, such as town squares. During the Baroque era space came to be recognised as infinite and this was given visual recognition by long perspective views which seemed to lead into infinity, and by the curved arrangement of columns and buildings so that their termination took place outside the field of vision, thus counteracting any idea of finite space. This impression of infinite space held good only for so long as the observer moved in well-defined, pre-ordained tracks; the slightest deviation would destroy the illusion of infinity. But the notion of moving along formal paths only is unacceptable to us. Spatial relationships must be accessible from any angle, by any route we choose. Due to our greater knowledge of the workings of nature and our political and social beliefs, this spatial freedom, expressed in architecture in Corbusier's Law Courts, is a prerequisite of our new urban environment. Each successive stage in the development of our spatial awareness is not replaced but is retained and built upon and contributes to a cumulative sensitivity to space. We may compare this process to the development of a human being during which basic instincts and emotions are not left behind as the individual develops, but continue to exert an influence, as part of the now richer and more complex personality. We must not think that because our appreciation of space is now so refined that the earlier attitudes do not apply any more; they are still within us and require satisfaction. In a modern town the instincts which produced

1

Medieval, Renaissance and Baroque visualisations should still be allowed to exert their creative influence, but, since times have changed, not in their original form.

The desire to be in a tightly tailored environment, to experience the spaceless sensation of enclosure, is still part of the human personality. Narrow lanes and small rooms are still a human need; they give comfort, and, when required, solitude; one can enter into close relations with certain other human beings, whether shopkeepers, friends, or strangers. But we also have the need to feel part of something larger than our own individualities or than this small group of people. An open civic space will normally fill this need—a space in which all the elements are related in a spatially relevant way, in which we can move about both as individuals, and as members of the community. Here the larger concepts of the community are symbolised by larger buildings and spaces, so that the individual can measure his own frame against the scale of the community. But this does not exhaust our requirements, for we also want to be reminded of the world outside our own community, we want to feel, and even see, the ties with others, the proximity of lines of communication or the open country.

These are crude distinctions, and in reality the gamut of spatial awareness is more gradual, rather like the succession of scenes described at the beginning of this book. We also recognise that a large civic complex, with its surrounding cellular structure, like the one in Venice, does in fact cater for all these human needs, and it is this which makes it so thoroughly satisfying. The narrow streets with their small communities and enclosed spaces, the arcades and their shops, the open piazza and other civic spaces, the sea with its boats and distant views, all these combine to form a truly humane environment, an involved mechanism designed to satisfy a vast range of human needs and moods, to serve the ends of individual and community alike.

3

4

6

Living in a town should add to the richness of each person's life and stimulate the different sides of his character.
A walk through a town like Bath allows one to experience this in physical and spatial terms.

*We enter the square in front of the entrance to Bath Abbey through a colonnade, **1**. As we advance into the square, **2**, we notice two openings, one on the left, a gap between the Abbey and other buildings through which we can see the open country, and another on the right which is however not wholly visible at this stage. We turn into this opening, **3**, and into another large square, **4**, of which the Abbey forms one side, **5**. We now cross this large open space and enter a short side street, **6**, at the end of which another much smaller square appears, **7**. This is almost completely filled by a huge old tree. A narrow, dark alley runs off to the left, **8**. Between two coarse textured walls we see, at the bottom, a much more elegant house. In the square itself there are many different shops, **9**, all of them highly individual, yet fitting into the harmonious pattern of the square. Consider the immense, rich variety of this sequence, from tight enclosure, **8**, to open spaces, **5**; the continuous promise of something not fully disclosed, for example, the countryside in **2**, the large building in **8**; the diversity of houses and shops, of light and shade.*

9

We have spoken of town design as a task of immense complexity, and this refers not only to the mechanical and social complexities, but also to the emotional ones. A group of buildings, or the spaces between them, may serve purely functional purposes but they may 'feel' wrong; a shape may seem too coarse, a space may induce feelings of claustrophobia or conversely of excessive exposure. The atmosphere emanating from a town cannot be created by wholly rational means; *it is nothing short of artistic expression*. In his role of artist the town designer must use his data creatively, in much the same way as the architect uses tables and statistics, and the potter uses his more empirical information about the properties of materials and the functions of his products.

Einstein once wrote that words are not always sufficient to carry the most advanced thought—they did not, in fact, play a very important part in his thought mechanism. He thought in terms of visual elements; he resorted to words only in the later stages of reasoning. At the other extreme of the human personality, the emotions, visual elements are felt by each one of us to be the most expressive and efficient forms of 'emotional thinking'. The deepest levels of our emotional lives are laid bare in dreams where, as Freud recognised, they are expressed in visual elements. Only rarely does a verbal idea enter into a dream. It is as though the two extremes of the human personality—the most profound thought and the most profound emotions— if projected beyond their normal scales, meet in the uncertain region where conscious and subconscious fuse. In this area the human mind does not function in words, which are too narrowly defined, but in visual elements which precede the formation of words and which are more suited to the multiplicity of meanings which abound in this region. The use of words manifests itself at the highest level as literature; the highest achievement in the use of visual elements is attained in the visual arts. This is why the visual arts, standing astride thought and feeling, probably command a greater slice of the human personality than the other arts. Town design, which is a distillation of all the visual arts, has in addition a physical environmental impact on us; for most of us it is the most powerful of the influences which shape our lives.

We must remember these points when, over the years, we make a great number of small decisions which will cumulatively decide the shape of tomorrow's towns. It would be foolish to copy the methods of the past, but we ignore the lessons of the past at our peril. After all we are still facing the same problem—the creation of a mechanically and emotionally efficient machine for living in.

1

2

3

A certain measure of control—or self-control—has always been one of the accepted tools of town building, so long as the town was recognised as a suitable expression of the community it contained and as a work of art. This control could take many different forms, conscious and unconscious. The harmonious pattern of the Grand Place in Arras, **2**, was the result of fairly strict civic laws which were imposed from the 17th century on. The Piazza della Signoria in Florence, **1**, page 160, also had controls imposed on it, but as can be seen in this picture the subtler, artistic methods of town building are stressed. The relationship of architecture and sculpture and the civic spaces created by them was left in the hands of artists. We can see that not only were they spatially related but they also took their place in the town's pattern of light and shade. The fact that they all look so brilliantly at their best in the lighting they receive—the medieval lions, Cellini's Perseus, Giambologna's dramatic, High-Renaissance group—and make such a potent contribution to the general pattern of light and shade of the townscape puts their joint effect beyond mere chance. This is the result of instinctive design and artistic awareness, which could never have been contrived or justified by rational means.

Such humane town designing came to an end with the Industrial Revolution. The apparent planning at Oldham, **3**, was in fact planlessness. Developments were easiest to handle in this pattern; immediate problems were minimised. But the real problems have been inherited by us in terms of human misery and inefficiency increased by a century of compound interest.

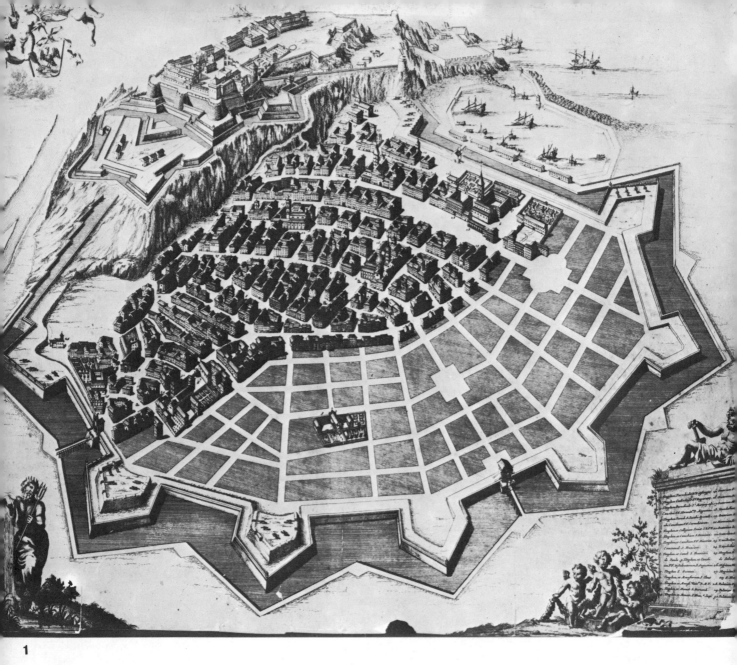

1

Towns have always had to adapt themselves to changing
conditions, and their growth has been controlled by political,
social and visual values, as demonstrated by the map of Nice **1**.
The castle has its own walls, and it is also partly protected by
the sheer cliff. Below, successive stages in town development are
distinguishable in the town pattern. The irregular medieval town
is followed by the more regular Renaissance extensions which
betray more awareness of space, and finally the Baroque
additions with their strict geometric pattern of streets and squares
and their scientifically designed ramparts. Each period speaks its
own visual language. Later town extensions did not as a rule
merge quite so smoothly with the existing structure of the town.
During the Industrial Revolution the older parts of towns were
generally blighted. During the 20th century even industrial
appendages of towns have been overtaken by their own
reorganisations and re-developments. In this picture of an
industrial suburb of San Francisco, USA, **2**, the original pattern of
roads and factories is still visible underneath the new system of
elevated junctions and overpasses which is completely unrelated to it.